16-20-04 (A 42-2021)

ENGLISH WHIGGISM

AND THE

AMERICAN REVOLUTION

ENGLISH WHIGGISM

AND THE

AMERICAN REVOLUTION

by G. H. Guttridge

UNIVERSITY OF CALIFORNIA PRESS
BERKELEY AND LOS ANGELES   1963

University of California Press
Berkeley and Los Angeles, California

Cambridge University Press
London, England

*Originally published in 1942 as Volume 28 of
the University of California Publications in History*

Second Printing, 1963
Manufactured in the United States of America

PREFACE

THIS ESSAY, published twenty years ago and long unavailable, is reprinted with only a few corrections. The alternative would have been to write a completely new book taking fully into account the considerable number of later works dealing with aspects of the subject. Such a book would have gained vastly in amplitude; and at some points the emphasis would have been different. More space would have been given to the "confederation of clans" which made up the Rockingham strength; to local politics, especially in Yorkshire; and to the relations between the Rockingham party and its potential allies in the City of London and in the Association movement of 1780. It is improbable, however, that the main conclusions would have been substantially changed.

G. H. G.

CONTENTS

I. THE WHIG TRADITION

WHIGGISM and toryism can be explained but not defined, and the appropriateness of the terms is often a matter of opinion. They arose in the twilight of a political order based on religious sanction, and they flourished before the concept of organized change had emerged. Thus they represent an intermediate stage between religious creeds and political programs. The creeds were vague, but the programs not yet positive. Individuals and groups were differentiated neither by religious belief nor by systems of policy, although both might play a part. The division between whig and tory was rather in temperament and interpretation of society.

Its essence lay in antithesis. In the seventeenth and eighteenth centuries the basis of controversy over the nature of government might be religious, political, or legal. It might emphasize the law of God, the law of nature, or the English constitution. In any event, the tory would find reason to justify unity and authority, the whig to assert particular rights. The law of God might ordain a king; it might also restrain the exercise of his power. The law of nature might presuppose monarchical government; it might also sanction revolution. The laws and customs of England could confer a broad prerogative; they provided also the precedents of Magna Carta and the Bill of Rights. Whig and tory alike drew upon the theories of the Middle Ages and the Reformation, modifying and transforming them until the Victorian Age of political democracy preferred a new terminology. The starting point for any discussion of whiggism under George III must therefore be that antithesis which distinguished "the opposite pillars of the constitution: the one vigilant lest government start into despotism; the other, lest it sink into anarchy."[1]

In face of the conflicting claims of liberty and order, toryism tended to regard the state much as the medieval theorist regarded the unity of Christendom. The whole was greater than its parts, and the nation than the sum of individuals or groups or interests. Each class and each individual had an appointed place in a noncompetitive scheme of society. Each had a special function and a special responsibility. The

[1] *Town and Country Magazine*, 1778, p. 24.

crown was both the symbol and the agent of this unity. Fortified by the authoritarian concepts of Roman law and by the unique opportunity of the English Reformation, the Stuart kings asserted the lofty ideal of a monistic state personified and directed by an anointed king. The incompetence of Stuart administration weakened but did not destroy the great ideal; and it emerged from civil war as the tory tradition.

There was an obvious and necessary alliance between toryism and the state church. Standing for the two great tory principles, national unity and a religious sanction for the established order, the Church of England was the central institution of toryism—the state in its religious aspect, and the divine principle in monarchical government. There can be no doubt that the body of clergy in the Church of England held tory principles in overwhelming measure, while the dissenters were as naturally inclined in the other direction.

If the Church as an institution was tory, so also was the rural community in which the parson shared preponderant control with the squire. There, at its best, was the solid, orderly, and unchanging society so dear to the tory heart. Before the Industrial Revolution the face of England was characteristically that of innumerable communities of this kind, with the squire or "country gentleman" as landlord, drawing his livelihood from his rent roll, and regarding his little community as hardly less real a natural unity than the nation itself. The manor house and the church were local centers of the tory creed, remote from London, having little concern with trade or finance, and maintaining some sense of obligation and some values other than those of money. The country gentleman was the opposite of the court gentleman, and he looked to the county, with its important local offices and its well-defined social structure, from which he might aspire to the most respected of parliamentary positions, that of member for the county, or knight of the shire. Local government consisted of unpaid services; and, relying on this inherent structural limitation of central authority, the tory disliked more positive attempts to restrict royal power. To such gentlemen as these the crown was the great symbol of the larger unity of the nation; but, as Professor Namier has said, although they worshiped the throne they loathed the court;[2]

---

[2] L. B. Namier, *England in the Age of the American Revolution* (London, 1930), p. 210.

and they aspired to forms of government in which the jobbery and favoritism of the capital should have no place. With all its emphasis on the crown, toryism was the creed of the English countryside.

The country gentleman was the local embodiment of a toryism which emphasized the religious sanction for a state based upon national unity. He feared the local tyranny and the national disintegration which might follow a revival of feudal privilege; he opposed religious diversity and sectarian organization; he suspected commercial and financial interests; and these, the disuniting or sectional elements in society, were the normal components of whiggism. Old feudal liberties, new financial opportunities, and Calvinistic separatism, however alien to one another, were still more alien to the harmonious structure of the tory ideal, and gravitated to the motley whig camp. "I scarce ever knew a foreigner settled in England," wrote a pamphleteer early in the eighteenth century, "whether of Dutch, German, French, Italian or Turkish growth, but became a whig in a little time after his mixing with us."[3]

Whiggism arose to combat the practical manifestations of toryism. From the Middle Ages it derived theories and experience, not of ordered unity, but of contractual obligation and restricted authority. In the seventeenth century it challenged the king. The combined authority of crown and church, as it was exercised by the early Stuarts, threatened the property and privileges of men active in politics, religion, and trade. These men had a platform for their opposition in parliament, the third great institution of the state. Here, with the assistance of political thinkers, they built a theory of government which would fit the practical necessities of their position—the limitation of royal power and the ultimate justification of resistance.

The driving force of whiggism, in and out of parliament, was in large measure the energy of the financial and commercial classes, linked closely with religious dissent. But actual leadership came not so much from the merchants as from the highest rank of the social and political hierarchy. The greater nobility in the eighteenth century formed a distinctive element in society, a class apart from the landed gentry

---

[3] *English Advice to the Freeholders of England,* quoted in *The State-Anatomy of Great Britain* (London, *ca.* 1717), p. 15.

although merging imperceptibly into it. Not only were they the owners of vast landed estates; they were regarded with an almost feudal respect, and perpetuated the ancient conception of the monarch as but the first among equals, "primus inter pares." "You," wrote Burke to one of them, "are the great oaks that shade a country, and perpetuate your benefits from generation to generation."[4] The great nobles, while sharing the country gentleman's passionate attachment to the rural estate, rarely refrained from participating also in the spoils of political influence. They were always torn between the temptations of the court and the pride of local power; and, being proud enough and powerful enough to resist the crown, might well become its most persistent rival. The alliance between such a nobility, jealous of royal power, and the religious dissenters, fearful of an established church, was indeed somewhat unnatural; but Disraeli was perhaps not far from the truth when he denounced it as the origin of the whig party, that "anti-national party" which was to him the enemy of all great national institutions.[5] At any rate, over against the basic homogeneity of toryism in crown, church, and countryside, whiggism emphasized the feudal ambitions of a greater nobility, the financial interests of a merchant class, and the sectarianism of religious dissent.

The division of outlook between whig and tory was reflected in foreign and economic policies. Whig interests tended to be hostile to France, because of commercial rivalry, antipathy to the Roman Catholic religion, and the fear of absolute government. Indeed, when partisan feeling ran high at a time of crisis in foreign affairs, opposition to the power of France might be regarded as the criterion of whiggism. Something may also be made of a tory tendency to national or imperial isolation, as against the profits of whig intervention in continental affairs. The tory country gentleman was more interested in a relatively free trade and less concerned in the protection of tariffs for the producer. But such divisions were not vital or consistent. They were the consequences rather than the characteristics of the two creeds, and it is dangerous to press them too far.

---

[4] *Correspondence of the Rt. Hon. Edmund Burke,* Earl Fitzwilliam and Sir Richard Bourke, eds. (London, 1844), I:381.
[5] *Vindication of the English Constitution* (1835), chap. xxx, reprinted in *Whigs and Whiggism* (London, 1913).

In 1689 the whigs were committed to revolution; and the principles of that revolution, formulated by Locke, became their gospel, and the foundation of English political thought in the eighteenth century. These principles had, of course, a direct relation to the claims put forward by the Stuart monarchy, and the antithesis of whig and tory creeds is seen clearly in that relation. The extreme assertion of royal power, as derived from God by a divine law overriding the rights of subjects, was met by the interpretation of divine law as a law of nature, according to which the function of authority was that of protecting the rights of individuals in a society wherein each acted on his own responsibility to God—a concept deriving largely from Calvinism and the French wars of religion, with their reasoned literature of resistance. According to Locke, men were naturally equal, in the sense that none had special rights of jurisdiction over others; and all had rights of life, liberty, and property, which the state existed solely to protect. Thus against the positive tory conception of the state the whigs visualized a negative function, to make possible the free play of individual and corporate energies in religion, politics, and trade.

In a society which was mainly an aggregation of individuals religion was the concern of the state only to the extent that its practices involved political action, as, for example, Catholic allegiance to a foreign power. A wide measure of toleration was thus an essential part of whiggism, and even after the middle of the eighteenth century it was possible to define the difference between whig and tory in religious terms, the whigs being "generally composed of the more moderate churchmen, and the main body of protestant dissenters."[6] The dissenters were in fact predestined whigs. They not only sympathized with whiggism; they represented one of its basic principles, the right of individuals to follow their own convictions in matters of religion, the institutions of which were purely voluntary. This right of independence was freely accepted by sympathetic churchmen. One of the sturdiest champions of whiggism, appointed to the chair of divinity at Cambridge in 1771, declared: "I had no prejudice against, no predilection for, the Church of England; but a sincere regard for the Church of Christ, and an insuperable objection to every degree of dogmatical

---

[6] *The Balance: or the Merits of Whig and Tory* (London, 1753), p. 4.

intolerance."[7] In theory and in practice whiggism was the creed of the dissenters, and as late as 1772 those who claimed its mantle were still referring to the dissenters as "that weighty body of men . . . who all over England are very powerful and who stick pretty much together," and whose "religious principles and our political ones are very similar, and most probably will make us generally act together."[8]

The interpretation of political society in accordance with the law of nature was a sufficient answer to the claim of an overriding divine sanction for the authority of king and church. But the law of nature was also embodied in the English constitution, as interpreted by whig apologists, and many precedents could be drawn from the Anglo-Saxon kingship and from Magna Carta to justify the limitation of monarchy. "A real whig," said Lord Molesworth in 1705, "is one who is exactly for keeping up to the strictness of the true old Gothic constitution, under the three estates of king (or queen), lords and commons; the legislature being seated in all three together, the executive entrusted with the first, but accountable to the whole body of the people, in case of mal-administration."[9]

Thus the revolution was justified in the contractual nature of government the authority of which was conditional upon the protection of individual rights. It was not enough to assert that the king was bound by fundamental law. That law must be implemented by the right of resistance, and by a constitution of checks and balances with component parts preserving a "nice equipoise" agreeable to Newtonian mechanics. Locke had no desire to encourage irresponsible resistance to authority; and the way of safety lay in parliamentary procedure. A representative legislature was essential to the whig program, and the separation of executive from legislative power seemed an equally desirable constitutional principle. An independent parliament was the guarantee of limited monarchy. Parliament indeed, with its bickerings and divisions, and its long history of attempts to restrain the crown, seems to personify the Lockian state, an aggregation of individuals and rival groups, rather than the harmonious structure of the tory dream. Whereas to the tory the crown and the church symbolized

---

[7] *Anecdotes of the Life of Richard Watson* (London, 1817), p. 39.
[8] Earl of Albemarle, *Memoirs of the Marquis of Rockingham* (London, 1852), II:224.
[9] *The Principles of a Real Whig* (reprinted; London, 1775), p. 6.

national unity, the whig saw in parliament the nation itself in miniature.

The whig nation was not only a nation of individuals; it was also the embodiment of property. An effective check to arbitrary power could be maintained only if the rights of property were scrupulously observed. Property was the first line of defense. Its rights were sacred, beyond the reach of executive authority, and could be preserved through the parliamentary control of taxation. In the earlier stages of whiggism in the seventeenth century, when the struggle to restrain the crown had not yet developed into the assertion of parliamentary supremacy, great stress was laid upon the immunity of property from government, an immunity expressed in the special function of the House of Commons to grant taxes to the crown. As a recent writer remarks, "parliament in its taxing function was nothing more than an institutional crystallization of the sanction of property";[10] and it is noteworthy that during the American Revolution Pitt could proclaim that taxation was no part of the governing power.[11] The emphasis placed by Locke upon the right of property is a clear indication of the importance with which it was regarded in the defense of constitutional liberties against the crown. As the watchdog of property, parliament had a unique importance in the whig interpretation of government and society.

The Glorious Revolution of 1688 and the events which followed, up to the Hanoverian succession in 1714, propelled whiggism from theories of contractual resistance to the justification of parliamentary supremacy; and toryism was driven to reconsider its principles and alter its course. Revolution had been a practical necessity. By his attack on the protestantism of the Church of England, on the local power of the country gentlemen as magistrates, and on the customary limits of royal prerogative James II betrayed the cause of the tories. The Revolution was national, not partisan. None the less it was a triumph for whiggism, and the whigs turned it to good account. The attempt to conceal the fact of revolution resulted in but the thinnest of veneers. James, it is true, was declared to have abdicated, but this was poor

---

[10] F. D. Wormuth, *The Royal Prerogative, 1603–1649* (Ithaca, N. Y., 1939), p. 14.
[11] See below, p. 66.

compensation to offset the statement that he had broken the original contract between king and people and that the throne was vacant. Toryism was forced to swallow its beliefs, and though it made a brave show under Anne, the odds against it were too great and the Hanoverian succession set the seal upon its failure. Parliamentary monarchy had arrived, and toryism paid the price.

The first obvious consequence was the ascendancy of parliament—the institution best suited to promote whig interests—and the decline of the tory monarchy and church. The new monarchy, established by the grace of parliament, could not serve the tory conception of the crown, and in fact the new king became a whig. The church, too, had suffered. Attacked by the Catholic James, it had been forced to acquiesce in wooing the dissenters, and when the revolution was safely over they claimed their reward. Tory unity of faith was sacrificed to whig toleration, and, after a strenuous tory action in the last ditch, toleration came to stay. Thus, although there was little change in the feelings or the opinions of those who in church and countryside maintained the tory faith, the political expression of that faith was gravely impaired. Toryism was killed back to its roots in the country, and only time could produce a vigorous new growth.

Meanwhile the whigs consolidated their power. The long ministry of Sir Robert Walpole in the 'twenties and 'thirties marks the establishment of the whig system and a new phase in the history of English government. It marks also the second stage in the disruption of partisan alignments. Entrusted with the executive power of the Hanoverian monarchy, Walpole pursued a policy at once calculated to strengthen whig interests and to win the waverers. His administrative and fiscal reforms were not in any real sense partisan, but tariffs were adjusted to the benefit of industrial interests rather than those of the consumer. The steadfast pursuance of peace, the refusal to repeal the legal disabilities of dissenters, the reduction of the land tax—all these main items in the Walpolean system were taken from the program of toryism. The influence of the landed gentry in local affairs was studiously respected, and, a country squire who transferred to Westminster the administrative skill which he had developed in the affairs of his estate, Walpole himself could well pose as the leader of the center, rather than of extremists. Only thus, by refraining from all action which might arouse the latent strength of toryism in the country, could the whig minority establish its ascendancy in parliament. Having lost its institutions, toryism was fast losing its policy.

The political fame of Walpole rests not only on policy, but also on the system by which that policy was made effective. The relation between executive and legislature was not specified in the Revolution settlement, and indeed the mere substitution of one king for another was no small part of the revolution. Having achieved the change, parliament was not concerned to lay down a rigid constitution; and there was serious friction between crown and parliament—that is, between executive and legislature—under both William and Anne. Many members still regarded their function of legislation as separate and distinct from the administration of the realm, and the "independence" of the House of Commons was their great ideal. With the accession of George I, however, the growth of ministerial power introduced a new element. To a large extent the executive powers of the crown were exercised by ministers who needed the confidence of both king and parliament—and the machinery of cabinet government was not yet in existence. Walpole therefore used the great resources of royal patronage to keep himself in office. He organized the system by which civil and military appointments were utilized to create a bloc in parliament sufficient to give a powerful advantage to the side of government. This system of "influence" was intricate in its manipulations and extended through those parts of the electorate and those members of parliament from which the greatest returns might be expected from the smallest outlay of favor. Under Walpole and the Pelhams patronage made use of every possible channel to achieve its end. The church was an important sphere of influence. Tory as were its clergy, they found themselves under the jurisdiction of latitudinarian whig bishops, whose theology made up in breadth for what it lacked in depth. In the upper house the whig bishops might even decide a division; and gradually the gentle moisture of patronage percolated to humbler levels. The clergyman also could play his part for the whig interest, as the papers of the Duke of Newcastle show.[12]

---

[12] D. G. Barnes, "The Duke of Newcastle, Ecclesiastical Minister, 1724–54," *Pacific Historical Review*, III (1934):164–191.

This system marked the transition between government by the king and government by a parliamentary party. The king still chose his ministers, but he had now to consider the approval of parliament in a far greater degree than in the seventeenth century. Patronage was the means of achieving a measure of agreement. It could not maintain a minister whom the governing class was determined to oust, but it could give a majority to a minister who was not displeasing to the representatives of the electors. Thus while on the one hand ministers exercised the powers of the king, on the other they guided the acts of the legislature. This concentration of power led George II to remark that ministers were kings in England.[13]

Whiggism by the middle of the century had superseded its theories of resistance by the politics of power. It had now two aspects. To its old face of contractual government, limited executive authority, and a balanced constitution it had added the aspect of parliamentary administration, the dispensation of influence, the exercise by deputy of royal functions, and the leadership of the church. The opportunities of patronage converted feudal vigilance into aristocratic preserves; and the rights which Locke had so strenuously maintained against the crown were turned into the perquisites of the aristocracy. The right of property, emphasized against royal covetousness, was now the justification of vast landed estates and proprietary seats in parliament; the right of freedom of debate, jealously upheld against an encroaching prerogative, became the safeguard against an inquisitive public. Just so had the Stuart kings directed against the people those high claims of monarchy which the Tudors had wielded for the nation against the feudal nobility and the Roman church. The analogy was tempting, not least to the colonists in America.

The outline of whiggism was blurred by prosperity, and under Walpole's successors, the Pelhams, it seemed to be transformed into an oligarchy of great families, combining the exercise of ministerial power with the manipulation of parliament. More and more the legatees of the Glorious Revolution tended to regard its achievements as justifying also the imperceptible consolidation of aristocratic power. The reluctant revolutionaries of 1689 became the complacent conserva-

---

[13] Namier, *op. cit.*, p. 53.

tives of 1750, and to them whiggism stood less for the principles which had produced the Glorious Revolution than for the society which it had inaugurated. The process may be said to have reached its logical climax during the American Revolution. At that time Burke created a political philosophy of conservatism from the experience and orderly evolution of aristocratic leadership. In so doing he completed the transfer of supremacy from king to parliament and revived the ideal of a monistic state under the leadership of an aristocracy whose sanction was not unlike that previously claimed for the king. The less orthodox Josiah Tucker, still professing whig principles, went further, and introduced his treatise on government by a refutation of Locke himself as the proponent of an impossible radical theory, while simultaneously the apologist of a practical oligarchy.[14]

The whiggism of Locke contained possibilities of widely different emphasis. In its pronouncements against arbitrary government it asserted the contractual obligation of monarchy to preserve certain fundamental rights. It also proclaimed the responsibility of parliament and the property represented therein for the maintenance of the contract. This latter responsibility justified in whig eyes the steady growth of parliamentary power over a monarchy dwindling in effective resources during the eighteenth century. By the reign of George III it had attained a supremacy comparable only with that previously claimed by apologists of divine right. But to Locke parliamentary power was a means, not an end. Many of his disciples still accepted his belief in the independence of the legislature, and resented the ability of ministers to sap that independence by means of royal patronage. They approved the principle of constitutional checks and balances, a principle now in jeopardy. Such "old whigs" appeared under Walpole, and were not far from becoming a new country party against a whig court.[15] Their suspicions of a pseudo toryism, enshrined in parliamentary supremacy, were confirmed by a pacific policy toward France and a coolness to the dissenters. They might well claim more of the spirit

---

[14] *A Treatise Concerning Civil Government* (London, 1781), Pt. I, reprinted in R. L. Schuyler, ed., *Josiah Tucker: A Selection from his Economic and Political Writings* (New York, 1931). Tucker continued his attack in *Four Letters on Important National Subjects* (Gloucester, 1783), wherein he described Locke as now the idol of freethinkers and levelers (pp. 108–109).

[15] K. G. Feiling, *The Second Tory Party* (London, 1938), p. 26.

of Locke than the orthodox corps of Walpole, for they insisted that the all-important element in government was the preservation of fundamental rights, not the privileges of parliament. The divergence between this insistence on fundamental law and the assertion of parliamentary supremacy was a vital factor in the American Revolution.[16]

In Locke also could be found the basis for a yet more liberal interpretation of whiggism. The whig aristocracy entrenched in parliament was resting on the laurels of liberty in the negative sense of resistance to encroachment by the king upon established forms of government and the security of property. If it was possible to question the complete authority of parliament in maintaining fundamental rights, it was also possible to question the adequacy of a representative system which regarded property as more important than persons. Locke had emphasized the ultimate sanction of government in "the people"; and "the people" had been interpreted as a select minority, a propertied class. The people of Britain, wrote Dr. John Brown in 1765, in their collective body comprised "the landed gentry, the beneficed country clergy, many of the more considerable merchants and men in trade, the substantial and industrious freeholders or yeomen."[17] The authority of such an interpretation was precarious, and it was challenged under George III by an appeal to the contractual rights of others than the oligarchy. English radicals and American colonists alike appealed to Locke, as political protestants to the bible of whiggism. Orthodox whigs, however, had no intention of giving birth to a philosophy of change. "The abstract right of the people," wrote Richard Watson in 1782, " . . . was exercised at the revolution; and we trust that there will never, in this country, be occasion to exercise it again."[18] A favorite whig toast in the 'eighties ran thus: "May the example of one revolution prevent the necessity of another!"[19] But the principles of 1689 contained no provision for a conflict between the actual English constitution and the law of nature upon which it rested.

While in the country the distinctions of whig and tory were becom-

---

[16] For the basic issues here involved see C. H. McIlwain, *Constitutionalism and the Changing World* (New York, 1939); *Constitutionalism, Ancient and Modern* (Ithaca, N. Y., 1940).

[17] *Thoughts on Civil Liberty* (London, 1765), p. 87.

[18] *Miscellaneous Tracts* (London, 1815), II:346.

[19] Rules and membership of the Whig Club, instituted May, 1784.

ing blurred by the implications of parliamentary government, in parliament itself the whigs were paying the price of success. There were too many mouths to feed, and the main corps, by 1750 under Newcastle, was challenged by rebel groups, often referred to as "parties." These groups called themselves the "friends" of some great personage, and when George Grenville told Newcastle that he had no friends[20] he was making a definite and intelligible political statement. Similarly when under George III a group began to call itself the "king's friends," that in itself is enough to indicate that the king might be regarded as a political leader within the accepted system of personal groups.

Such were the consequences of the whig monopoly. By 1760 whiggism had become so much the system of power that it had lost the distinguishing marks of its origin. On the one hand, it had absorbed the tory crown and church, while toryism had been obliged to accept the revolution settlement. There were no clear lines of demarcation. On the other hand, to make the confusion complete, whiggism itself had broken up into groups. Pamphleteers and orators, and presumably the public at large, included old creeds and new groups in one general condemnation, and it became the fashion to denounce an undefined and indeterminate thing called "party," which was regarded as the source of political evils, or at least as the outward sign of the political degradation of a degenerate age.

The appearance of these personal groups proved the salvation of toryism. Gradually, under the guidance of Bolingbroke and Windham, the tories had accepted the inevitable. They had reconciled themselves to the Revolution settlement, the Hanoverian succession, and a modicum of religious toleration. Their creed had lost the bloom of its monarchical sentiment and the moral fiber of its religious sanction, but it still retained its concept of the state as something more than an aggregation of individuals, of sectional interests, or of "parties."

It is one of the paradoxes of political history, in the century before the appearance of organized government by party, that the very idea of party is a partisan idea. Toryism at its best could not admit the division of the state which such a system implies. Toryism, that is,

[20] Namier, *op. cit.*, p. 351.

was the creed of the nonpartisan state. It was in this guise that it returned under Pitt and George III; and the recognition of this fact
makes more intelligible the shifting negotiations which followed 1760.
In this sense the new reign inaugurated a tory revival, and in this sense
the history of party was continuous. Toryism had lost its divinely
ordained monarchy and its religious comprehensiveness, but it need
not for that reason forego its ideal of unity. Under a Hanoverian king
who "gloried in the name of Britain" the form was different but the
principle was the same. The difference of form and circumstance,
however, accounts for the fact that the new toryism did not by any
means include the same persons who called themselves tories in 1760.
Tories submerged for forty years by the whig tide might well come
up on different sides of the ship.

The tory attack on party could take advantage of a long-standing
dissatisfaction with the complacent patronage and the unscrupulous
self-seeking of political groups. The average member of parliament
was no prophet. He could not discern the future justification of Walpole's system as building a bridge between executive and legislature
and ending the constitutional deadlock which had seemed a virtue
to the whiggism of the Revolution. He was apt to make ineffective
protests against the loss of legislative independence, and to look with
favor on a program designed to reduce competition for the spoils of
office. And so, when Bolingbroke had persuaded the majority of tories
to accept the established parliamentary monarchy, he proceeded to
go farther and denounce the system of patronage and "parties." This
nonpartisan crusade was the favorite theme of his political writings,
and has become famous through the "Patriot King."[21] Whatever be
the indebtedness of George III to this work, there can be little doubt
that the opinions which it formulated made his influence the greater.

The principle of the nonpartisan state, and the practical attack on
ministerial patronage, had a more formidable champion than Bolingbroke. William Pitt emerged from the rebel whigs who challenged the
orthodox interest of Walpole and Newcastle. His whiggism was of
that ancient order which believed in the restraint of government by

---

[21] H. N. Fieldhouse, "Bolingbroke and the Idea of Non-Party Government," *History*,
Vol. XXIII, No. 89 (June, 1938).

law, and he never accepted the full implications of parliamentary supremacy over king or people. In this respect his ideas were akin to those of Bolingbroke. Whereas the doctrine of governmental restraint by fundamental law had been in the seventeenth century a whig doctrine used to challenge the supremacy of the king, in the eighteenth it would naturally appeal to tories or radicals seeking to restrain the new supremacy of a whig parliament.

Nor did Pitt accept the practical necessities which accompanied parliamentary supremacy. He attacked patronage as corruption, and party as faction. He rallied to his side a miscellaneous band of patriots and rebels whose adherence weakened the orthodox whig magnates. The tories supported him rather than buttress Newcastle's whig machine. The merchants found in him a sympathetic political leader, far more congenial in upbringing and in understanding than the great whig lords whose commercial interests were traditional rather than real. With the merchants and the City of London, Pitt tended also to attract the more radical elements in English politics, and he remained closer to the radical point of view than any other political leader. By appropriating the commercial and the liberal supporters of whiggism, and adding to them many tory country gentlemen, Pitt became the potential leader of a group which could challenge the supremacy of the old whig system. While he thus prepared the way for the policy of George III, he himself remained the rival champion of nonpartisan policy, and when the new king attempted a similar leadership he found to his cost that Pitt was already in possession.

The position of Pitt as a nominal whig occupied in clearing the way to a new toryism completes the confusion of 1760, and many historians have denied all validity to the names of whig and tory in the succeeding period. Whiggism in power was very like toryism. The most effective opposition to it came from rebel "parties" also professing the whig name. Ministry and opposition were alike whig; so also were conservative and liberal. Is there not therefore an essential unreality in the preservation of the old names? It might be so, but for two important facts. The first is the reappearance of the king as a personal force in politics. Whether or not the accession of George III has any constitutional significance, it undoubtedly made a practical difference. The king became an active participant in politics. He attempted to dissolve parties, and his chosen ministers associated his government with an illiberal and authoritarian policy which made John Wilkes and the American colonies the centers of violent controversy. On the other side, a group of whigs championed the waning cause of liberty and developed a systematic opposition. Once more, as under the Stuarts, the advocates of authority and the nonpartisan state were challenged by the champions of individual and corporate rights, organized in some degree as a party. This new antithesis is sufficiently near the old to justify the transference of the old terms, and they were actually so transferred. The difficulty for the historian lies in the fact that there is no necessary relation between the alignments of individuals or groups before and after 1760. Toryism was not restored, but re-created; and whiggism took up again the weapons of resistance.

II. THE ROCKINGHAM WHIGS

WHEN George III came to the throne, national harmony and a national government still seemed the normal political procedure, and Goldsmith expressed a widespread feeling when he wrote:

> But when contending chiefs blockade the throne
> Contracting regal power to stretch their own,
> When I behold a factious band agree
> To call it freedom when themselves are free ...
> ... half a patriot, half a coward grown,
> I fly from petty tyrants to the throne.[1]

This was the opportunity of the new reign. Already William Pitt had shown how strong was the force which could rally behind a popular leader who was avowedly nonpartisan. The king had greater material resources, and he was determined to choose his own ministers, rather than accept a particular "set" whose parliamentary majority depended largely on control of royal patronage. In so doing, George III was unconscious of any innovation. He was a firm believer in the constitution of 1689, "the most beautiful combination that ever was framed."[2] Like Pitt, he tended to regard it as a fixed and permanent form of government, not dependent upon the changing will of a supreme legislature, and he seems to have believed that some statutes passed during the Revolution settlement could not be set aside by act of parliament.[3] Like Pitt also, he did not accept the whig monopoly as a legitimate part of the governmental system. While there is no evidence that he had any desire to increase the royal prerogative, George III was determined not to shirk his ultimate responsibility for the execution of government.

In order to follow the lines which he believed to be his duty, the new king needed to establish an orderly and stable administration on an equilibrium of three forces. His ministers must be politically congenial and personally acceptable to himself; they must have control of the

---

[1] *The Traveller* (1764).

[2] *Correspondence of King George III*, ed. Sir John Fortescue (London, 1928), Vol. V, No. 2991.

[3] D. G. Barnes, *George III and William Pitt* (Stanford Univ. Press, 1939), pp. 348, 480.

complicated machinery of influence; and they must be popular enough to carry some weight with the independent members of parliament, many of whom would give the ministry the benefit of any reasonable doubt. George III found Pitt in charge of policy and Newcastle in control of patronage. His accession was inevitably a signal for the increased fury of personal ambitions and factional jealousies, and the appointment of Lord Bute as minister, with special ties to the king, soon threw the government out of gear. Bute had neither popularity nor personal influence, but he had royal favor. What had been an uneasy coalition now became an impossible triumvirate. Before long first Pitt and then Newcastle resigned; and the king appointed more amenable ministers. Opposition was then proscribed by the dismissal of whig nominees, great and small, whose allegiance was too close to the corps of Newcastle. It remained only to satisfy the independent members of parliament. This Bute could not do. He gave way therefore to George Grenville, a minister less agreeable to the king but less obnoxious to parliament. By this concession to parliamentary whiggism the king obtained a precarious majority.

Confronted by this new situation, traditional whigs and tories could find equally good reasons for choosing support or opposition, according as they regarded one or the other of their ancient principles paramount. The tories could rally to the king, or, retaining their profound dislike of centralization and parliamentary jobbery, could refuse support to this semblance of monarchy. The whigs who retained their fears and jealousies of the crown could join an aristocratic opposition, but those who clung to the parliamentary preserve of a system traditionally whig might equally well accept the new king as their party leader.[4] Some of the old whig leaders were thus willing to remain on the new terms of sufferance; others went out. Some old tories rallied round the banner of supposedly nonpartisan monarchy, but they soon saw that the king was following very closely the whig technique of management, and many remained aloof. In 1762 the min-

---

[4] Cf. Anthony Trollope, *Doctor Thorne:* "There is a great difference in Whigs. Lord de Courcy was a Court Whig, following the fortunes, and enjoying, when he could get it, the sunshine of the throne. . . . The Duke of Omnium was a Whig of a very different calibre. He rarely went near the presence of majesty, and when he did so, he did it merely as a disagreeable duty incident to his position. He was very willing that the Queen should be queen so long as he was allowed to be Duke of Omnium."

isters commented that the great body of tories was by no means assured, and some were very much to the contrary.[5] Six years later many tories were in opposition, and at least one election was fought between two "king's friends" on one side and two tories on the other.[6] George III did not make the tories the basis of his power. Under the guise of a national government he unwittingly created a new party, and the term "tory" with its royalist associations was appropriately transferred to it. On the other hand, those who remained outside claimed the true reversion of the whig name, as against those whose whiggism stood only for the vested interest of ministerial power. But they were similarly mixed in ancestry. At least one of the leaders of the new "whig" opposition, William Dowdeswell, was a tory country gentleman who had in no discernible way changed his opinions or his policy. A new start had been made in the history of party, and, until a fresh political generation grew up, new and old existed together to confound the historian.

In his theoretically nonpartisan crusade, and his actual formation of a party, the king relied mainly on those seventy or eighty members who, in the customary usage of political groups, were christened the king's "friends." But this minority could form only the nucleus of a regular ministerial majority in parliament, and the shifting ministries of the first decade bear witness to the formation of this majority, essential to a strong and stable administration. One practical result of the king's policy, which was to have far-reaching effects in the history of party, was that in the process he alienated enough influential men to make a potential opposition. By 1763 some of these were already considering their position. The younger and more energetic proposed to meet regularly and confer as an opposition party, and in 1764 meetings were being held for dinner at Wildman's Tavern. These meetings seem at first to have included about 150 members of parliamentary groups outside the ministry, but the great whig leaders were perplexed by their proscription, and hesitated to take formal steps hitherto associated only with reckless rebel whigs. Moreover, there was no Prince of Wales to whose reversionary interest they might attach themselves

[5] Quoted in L. B. Namier, *England in the Age of the American Revolution* (London, 1930), p. 404.
[6] K. G. Feiling, *The Second Tory Party* (London, 1938), p. 74.

as previous oppositions had done; and the young king's uncle, the Duke of Cumberland, was an unsatisfactory substitute.[7] The numbers dwindled, and separated into their component groups. A breach seemed likely between the powerful landed nobility and those lesser whigs who must form the body of a party. At this critical stage Lord Rockingham stepped to the front. Young, and belonging to the "high whigs" of vast estates, he proceeded to exercise the one great gift which entitles him to a place among prime ministers, namely, that of reconciling individuals and inspiring an unusual devotion among a group of considerable size. A large number of whigs, especially the younger members of Newcastle's main corps, rallied round the new leader. Youth was a prominent feature of the movement; and although Rockingham never united all who claimed the name of whig, he did form the one connection worthy of comparison with that of the king, in numbers, unity, and political power.

By 1765 Lord Rockingham's friends included several of the wealthiest dukes and landowners and a large following of active party men. Almost at once they faced a crisis. The king had reached the limit of his endurance with George Grenville and needed other ministers to give support to his own "friends." For two months negotiations proceeded for a new government. The natural sequel would have been the formation of a coalition between Pitt and the various whig elements, especially those led by Rockingham. This, however, was frustrated, first by Pitt's insistence on control and later by Temple's refusal to provide support. The king made a hopeless effort to form a ministry without either Pitt or Rockingham; at the end of June he fell back on the main corps of the whigs. They on their side had to choose between returning to office or holding out for the surrender of the patriot king and a restoration of the old whig system. They chose the illuminating experiment of office.

They were manifestly not yet a party. Acceptance had been urged upon them by the Duke of Newcastle, who was anxious to snatch the unexpected opportunity of turning out the ministry he disliked. Other adherents of the old whig system believed that Rockingham made a

---

[7] Namier, *op. cit.*, pp. 484–485; *The History of the Late Minority* (third impression; London, 1766), pp. 297–300; *Letters from George III to Lord Bute, 1756–66*, ed. Romney Sedgwick (London, 1939), pp. xx, xlix.

fatal mistake in taking office without Pitt, whereas by refusing he could have forced George III to return to the comparative quiescence of his grandfather. In fact, the whigs assisted the king to tide over a difficult situation; and they were incapable of supporting office without substantial outside help. The royal Duke of Cumberland possessed influence and prestige in political rivalry with the king—a rivalry, like that of a Prince of Wales, punctuated by occasional and profitable reconciliations. The year 1765 was one of reconciliation, and upon Cumberland the young whigs relied.[8] They strained the bands of connection. They appealed to youth and kinship, persuading Lord Dartmouth to take office, and vainly attempting to retain Lord North. They included in the ministry some of the king's friends; they sought the coöperation of Pitt, and took in some of his allies; and they looked for help to those independent country gentlemen who had no liking for the new toryism. This probably accounts for the inclusion of two "old" tories in the ministry, one, William Dowdeswell, becoming chancellor of the exchequer.

Dowdeswell was a county member, with the prestige and pride that his position implies; and the Duke of Newcastle had lamented his appearance as a second tory for Worcestershire in 1761.[9] There is no indication until 1765 that he was consulted or included by the friends of Lord Rockingham, still less by the Duke of Newcastle. His name does not appear among the members of opposition dining at Wildman's Tavern, or at other meetings of whigs. Nor is his conduct in parliament conclusive, although by 1764 he was voting with the minority on some leading issues. He had come into prominence as the appropriate champion of the "cider counties" against the excise duties on cider and perry imposed in 1763 by the Bute ministry.[10] These impositions had been bitterly resisted by the western counties, and many of their representatives, tory though they might be, were willing to make common cause with the opposition. Newcastle attempted to organize a formid-

---

[8] Newcastle's *Narrative of the Changes in the Ministry, 1765–1767* (London, 1898), *A History of the Late Minority* (London, 1765–66), *The Principles of the Late Changes* (London, 1766); Sedgwick, *loc. cit.*

[9] Namier, *op. cit.*, pp. 131–132.

[10] William Dowdeswell, *An Address to Such of the Electors of Great Britain as Are Not Makers of Cyder and Perry* (1763), reprinted in *A Collection of Scarce and Interesting Tracts* (London, 1788).

able parliamentary attack on this basis, and although his friends were
not all willing to commit their connection to a regular alliance, there
was a temporary association which led some individuals to cross the
uncertain line dividing tory from whig. The agitation in the cider
counties was based upon grievances essentially local; but at the same
time John Wilkes was drawing the attention of the entire country
to similar issues of personal liberty threatened by invasions of the
executive power, and it is not surprising that Dowdeswell appeared
on the whig side when parliament took up the question of the legality
of general warrants. In both controversies the central point was the
alleged right of officials to investigate the homes of private persons.
Matters of trade and taxation made the post of chancellor of the exchequer one in which it was vital to have a trusted minister, preferably
one who would have the support of the landed gentry. What better
choice could there be than the champion of the traditionally faithful
"cider counties," and a man known and respected for his industry and
integrity? The new recruit was not one of the old corps, it is true, but
that corps was too small for an administration and must seek outside
help. The tory country gentleman who now took charge of whig
finance proved to be a faithful and competent leader of the future
party.[11]

Nothing in the history of the new administration was of greater
permanent significance than the appointment of Edmund Burke as
Rockingham's secretary in July. Brought into parliament five months
later by a patron friendly to Rockingham, Burke

> Born for the universe, narrowed his mind
> And to party gave up what was meant for mankind.[12]

He soon became the driving force of the ministry. With Dowdeswell
he worked to win back the full support of the merchants, who had
tended to go over to Pitt, and the attempt resulted in a working alli-

[11] One of Dowdeswell's first acts as a minister showed that he had not surrendered
to a faction. Sir Edward Winnington, an old friend of tory and Jacobite descent, had
been appointed to a minor post by Bute, after the dismissal of Newcastle's "innocents."
The new ministry now replaced him by their former protégé, whereupon Dowdeswell
appointed as his secretary the man whom Rockingham had dismissed, on the clear
understanding that Winnington might not always vote with the government.—Dowdeswell MSS in the William L. Clements Library.

[12] Oliver Goldsmith, *Retaliation* (1774).

ance with both the American and the West Indian trading interests.[13] This alliance showed its importance when American agitation against the Stamp Act became known in England.

American disturbances clamored for attention by December, and the ministry, divided and uncertain, delayed the announcement of a policy. The merchants of London organized a national agitation; and, true to the alliance he needed, but recognizing that any concession would face bitter opposition from the conservative members of his own group, as well as from the king, Rockingham supported the organization. He and Dowdeswell held several meetings with the representatives of the merchants and informed them that the right to tax America could not be surrendered, but that the act might possibly be suspended. Repeal was decided on at a meeting of five ministers, Rockingham, Grafton, Conway, Townshend, and Dowdeswell, on January 17th.[14] Petitions flowed in during the next two weeks; and in February the Declaratory Act was introduced, followed later in the month by the repeal of the Stamp Act. From this time on, Rockingham, Dowdeswell, and Burke shared the gratitude of the commercial interest, especially of the North American merchants, and worked to retain that alliance which was a peculiar feature of the Rockingham administration.

Important though it was, the repeal of the Stamp Act cannot be regarded as the main plank in the ministerial platform. It was merely one of several measures in which sound practical policy blended incalculably with the urgent necessity of gratifying all the sections of influential opinion which were disposed to support the whigs. The merchants formed one of these. The independent country gentlemen were less definite in their predilections, but at least those of the cider land had reason to look hopefully for relief to the member of their own group who was now chancellor of the exchequer. They did not look in vain. Dowdeswell regarded the repeal of the hated excise on cider as an important part of his duty. In March, 1766, he prepared for the government a careful memorandum, in which he recapitulated

---

[13] L. Stuart Sutherland, "Edmund Burke and the First Rockingham Ministry," *English Historical Review*, XLVII (1932):46–72.

[14] D. A. Winstanley, *Personal and Party Government* (Cambridge, 1910), p. 262.

the arguments of his earlier pamphlet and stressed the hardship which an excise placed on the small landowner, as against the liabilities of the merchant and trader, to whom such duties were in the nature of a normal expense or risk.[15] His policy was successful, and the duties of 1763 were repealed in favor of the older imposition upon retailers. Having thus satisfied the merchants and the country gentlemen, the ministry made a cautious bid for liberal support by declaring against general warrants; but already dissolution was at hand. The powerful patronage of Cumberland had ended with his death in the previous October. It was evident that Pitt could not be won over, and his friends, led by the Duke of Grafton, now deserted Rockingham. In July the ministry resigned.

Pitt at last took his place at the head of a nonpartisan administration the mosaic elements of which were to be immortalized by Burke. It was now the turn of Rockingham's friends, as before of Pitt's, to decide on their attitude to the ministry, with this difference, that the prestige of Pitt led him to assume that he had but to summon and they to obey. The Rockingham whigs thought differently, and trouble began with the chancellorship of the exchequer.

Among the many whigs who still clung to the vague and convenient tradition of whiggism rather than to a definite or coherent group was Charles Townshend. He had accepted the lucrative office of paymaster under Grenville; he had been considered for chancellor of the exchequer in later whig negotiations; and he had finally retained his position as paymaster under Rockingham without taking a prominent part in the ministry.[16] His friend Dowdeswell had been called to the exchequer, instead of playing a subordinate role on the treasury board under Townshend. Now, with the fall of the Rockingham administration Townshend and Dowdeswell came again into awkward proximity. Pitt had placed Grafton at the head of the treasury, and Grafton sought for Townshend as his chancellor. Pitt was more than doubtful and apparently would have preferred to retain "dull Dowdeswell," whom he regarded as a safe mediocrity. He acquiesced, however, in Grafton's preference, and the office was offered

---

[15] Add. MSS (Brit. Mus.) 35,879, fols. 345–353.
[16] Newcastle's *Narrative of the Changes in the Ministry, 1765–1767*, p. 25; Dowdeswell MSS.

to Townshend. The latter, torn between ambition and profit, could not make up his mind, while Pitt grew impatient and the whigs offended. "Every dissatisfied person," wrote Grafton to Pitt, "is endeavouring to persuade the duke of Portland, Dowdeswell, etc., that they are slighted by being left without any notion whether they are to be in or out." Townshend himself declared to the king that "Lord Rockingham being quiet would much depend on Mr. Dowdeswell's remaining Chancellor of the Exchequer."[17] Nevertheless, he decided to take the post, though he could not avoid a regretful glance back to the easy profits of the paymastership.

Dowdeswell was more stubborn. He had an interview with the king, who complimented him on his services and declared his intention of finding him a suitable place. Dowdeswell replied that it was sometimes a misfortune to have been raised too high, for one could not then stoop to lower places which might otherwise have been accepted. The hint was not taken. He was offered his choice between a joint paymastership with Lord North and the presidency of the board of trade, later given to Hillsborough. To the king's surprise, he declined both.[18] The significance of his conduct throughout the negotiations lies in the fact that in spite of expressed fears he would probably have accepted the higher post, in accordance with the policy of his friends, which was to retain as much solidarity as possible in the new ministry. The issue was one not only of personal pride, but of the pride of "Lord Rockingham's friends." The historian may be pardoned for speculating on the events which might have followed if Pitt had not allowed Grafton to put Townshend into the office from which he revived American unrest; and if, instead, Pitt's own choice of Dowdeswell had won a greater measure of confidence from the group which was to prove by far the most powerful whig corps.

Thus the Rockingham whigs, after less than a year in office, entered the political wilderness where they were to remain for sixteen years. During that time they became to a great extent a coherent and ex-

[17] *Correspondence of William Pitt, Earl of Chatham*, W. S. Taylor and J. H. Pringle, eds. (London, 1839), II:452–466; *Autobiography . . . of Augustus Henry, Third Duke of Grafton* (London, 1898), p. 92; D. A. Winstanley, *Lord Chatham and the Whig Opposition* (Cambridge, 1912), pp. 53–54.

[18] Dowdeswell MSS, some of which are printed in *Sir Henry Cavendish's Debates* (London, 1841), I:579–581.

clusive political party. At first their policy was uncertain and hesitating. For a few months they supported Pitt, now Earl of Chatham, and sought to retain as much influence and as many places in the ministry as he would allow. The Duke of Portland, for example, remained as lord chamberlain, in spite of his declared intention to act always as a servant of the Rockingham party.[19] This policy became less promising when Chatham dismissed some of their number from minor offices; and the group attempted to bring pressure on their remaining adherents in the ministry, headed by Conway, to resign in a body, thereby forcing Chatham to admit the need of party support. Conway, however, was suspicious of organized party. He hesitated and, in spite of the earnest solicitation of Portland, remained, although estranged from Chatham, and, as he himself declared, a "passenger" in the ministry.[20] Chatham's illness soon deprived his followers of all effective control. Townshend, who had continued to consult Dowdeswell for several months after succeeding him at the exchequer, led the ministry's American policy away from that of his former friends, and the Rockingham whigs were obliged to turn elsewhere for the help necessary to gain power.

They considered the obvious union with the Bedford whigs, who were willing to join in unqualified opposition to the influence of Lord Bute. For a while the two groups found themselves working together in opposition to a ministry which was passing out of Chatham's hands, and in the summer of 1767 there was the brief prospect of a joint administration under Rockingham. The chief obstacle to a firm alliance was the position of Grenville, with whom the Bedford whigs were now in close association. Grenville's American policy had been repudiated by the Rockingham ministry, and, directly or indirectly, this obstacle prevented the success of the whig reunion which Newcastle so ardently desired.[21] "Making Mr. Grenville minister would be the most inconsistent act for us that could be thought of," Rockingham declared, "and . . . we, who were determined to act con-

---

[19] A. S. Turberville, *A History of Welbeck Abbey and Its Owners* (London, 1939), II:91–92.

[20] Winstanley, *Lord Chatham and the Whig Opposition*, p. 85.

[21] *Anecdotes of the Life of the Rt. Hon. William Pitt, Earl of Chatham* (London, 1793), II:121–125.

sistently, would never join in such a plan."[22] Portland agreed with this view. Dowdeswell appears to have been slightly more conciliatory to a junction with Grenville than his leader, but his attempt at reconciliation was, as he wrote to Lady Rockingham, without much success. "It was abrupt, and G. G. must pave the way for me by *proper submissions,* before I can hope for success."[23] The difficulty of Grenville's past actions and policy prevented union, the negotiations broke down, and in November, 1767, Grenville made a public repudiation of the Rockingham whigs through Dowdeswell and declared his refusal to act with them.[24]

In this confused period from 1766 to 1770 the concept of party grew slowly. Loyalty to the group was a principle congenial to aristocracy at its best, and the principle was formulated in word and deed. In 1767 Rockingham and his friends were tempted to increase their parliamentary power by so doubtful an expedient as Dowdeswell's successful motion to reduce the land tax; but this brought significant protests from influential leaders, who believed that a coherent party must rest on a foundation of principle. "Never let us drive a wrong or a dubious point," Sir George Savile urged Rockingham, "because we have numbers."[25] The same year Rockingham defined the two fundamental principles of the party. "Our first principle," he wrote to Dowdeswell, "was, that Lord Bute's power was dangerous, and therefore was to be resisted: our second arose from Mr. George Grenville's conduct as minister, whose measures and opinions were opposed, and afterwards corrected; and therefore consistency requires that we should never aid to throw government into his hands." It was necessary, he went on, to fix acknowledged principles in the minds of all, to avoid the imputation of private interest. The maintenance of character and credit was necessary and, in spite of appearing at times a forlorn hope, might well prove to be the best policy. Two years later, Rockingham was still urging the same need. "We should constantly look back," he wrote, ". . . and adhere to the same line in future. I think we, and

---

[22] Earl of Albemarle, *Memoirs of the Marquis of Rockingham* (London, 1852), II: 32; *Cavendish's Debates,* I:581–582.

[23] Dowdeswell MSS (Mar. 20, 1768); *Cavendish's Debates,* I:582.

[24] Winstanley, *Lord Chatham and the Whig Opposition,* pp. 187–188.

[25] Albemarle, *op. cit.,* II:36.

we only, of all the party now in opposition, are so on system and principles. . . . We should be cautious not even to throw the appearance of leading into hands whose principles we have no reason to think similar to our own."[26]

The real test came in 1769. During the previous year several events had occurred to create an essentially different political situation. The election of 1768, it is true, had brought no material change, but the followers of Bedford had been admitted as a group into the ministry, thus putting an end to the prospect of union in opposition and leaving the Rockingham whigs with little chance of forcing their way back to power. On the other hand, the Bedford group reinforced that section of the ministry most alien to Chatham, and before long the friction was so great that Chatham and Shelburne resigned from office. From now on the practical problem of whig politics was the relation between Chatham and Rockingham. There were, however, two other significant changes. American policy was urgent, for the Townshend duties of 1767 had added fuel to colonial unrest, and with Chatham and Shelburne out of the ministry, and the Bedfords in, the line of demarcation between the American policy of the ministry and that of opposition became far clearer than for several years past. Finally, the election of 1768 brought Wilkes once more to the front and raised issues of electoral rights and parliamentary freedom, on which the whigs could make a gallant fight. In the persons of Wilkes and others the ministry, spurred on by the king, had previously attacked the freedom of the press and the right of free speech in parliament, and had allowed such controversial subjects as general warrants and the laws of libel to place the government in an illiberal and aggressive position. To these was now added the attack on the right of electors to return members of their own choosing.

In February the storm broke. Wilkes was expelled for a libel on the ministry and declared incapable of sitting in the House of Commons. This arbitrary proceeding was opposed even from within the ministry by Conway and Dunning, and George Grenville found himself fighting by the side of the Rockingham phalanx. In April the House went farther and seated Wilkes's unsuccessful opponent, Colonel Luttrell,

---

[26] *Cavendish's Debates,* I:585.

for Middlesex. The outraged county petitioned and led a stream of petitions from towns and counties, varying only in the degree of their hostility to the ministerial majority. The whigs now had a great cause. The raw material of opposition was amply present, and the apparent challenge to constitutional rights was taken up by various groups and persons, more or less principled, demanding a variety of remedies for the common complaints—"complaints of such an impression that for the pattern of them we must go back beyond the Revolution."[27] One of the reformers declared long afterward that the Middlesex election had been a principal cause of the American Revolution; for after such high-handed action by the House of Commons the Americans could no longer consider parliament as the representative of the people, but must regard its members as the packed adherents of a profligate ministry in whom it would be idle to invite American confidence.[28]

The controversies which raged during the first three years of the new parliament are of the greatest significance for an understanding of English politics in the American Revolution. The issue was the authority of parliament, and particularly of the House of Commons. The House asserted its right to determine the eligibility of persons elected to it, to declare their incapacity, and now to select as member for the county of Middlesex a candidate who had received only a small number of the votes cast. While thus asserting its authority over the electorate, the House was greatly concerned over the publication of its debates and over alleged libels contained therein. In all these matters it strove to preserve against the electorate those privileges which had originally protected it against the king. The struggle developed into a violent conflict between representatives in parliament and a section of the electorate which they were presumed to represent—"a situation new and extraordinary in this Government," declared the Yorkshire petition, "the Representation of the People in opposition to the People." "There is a time," the Lord Mayor of London announced to the king, "when it is morally demonstrable that men cease to be representatives. That time is now arrived: the present House of Commons do not represent the people." "There are now two parties," said Burke,

---

[27] *A Fair Trial of the Important Question* ... (London, 1769), p. 241.
[28] *Parliamentary History*, XXII:100–101.

"one for the representatives, the other in support of the rights of the people against the representatives."[29]

In this contest the principles of whiggism were ranged on both sides. From Locke came an insistence on the separation of executive and legislature which had been deemed a necessary restraint of tyranny. This separation of powers in a system of constitutional checks and balances had been magnified by Montesquieu and others to become the central safeguard of liberty. It was now interpreted by the constitutionalism of George III and the legalism of Blackstone to emphasize the form of government at the expense of its spirit, and to protect the legislature from its critics in the country. The authority of parliament had been the watchword of whiggism since the Revolution, and those who chose to disregard its remoteness from popular consent could urge the House of Commons to exert itself in support of its rightful powers, which, they said, the people had been repeatedly called upon to unite against and withstand. "It is our business," declared Charles Fox for the ministry in 1771, "to act constitutionally and to maintain the independency of parliament: whether it is attacked by the people or by the crown is a matter of little consequence."[30]

But what, meanwhile, of that Lockian whiggism which had maintained the rights of individuals, expressed through their representatives, against the state, the function of which was to preserve them? This aspect of whiggism had come near to asserting the sovereignty of the majority. The cleavage was ominous and recalled the fact that patronage had clogged the channel through which the representative received the consent of the electorate. As controversy developed, and the king became more obviously associated with the system of patronage, it was easy for critics to detect and to denounce a new toryism still professing whig principles.

The position of Chatham was clear. He had already opposed the perversion of the constitution through ministerial patronage. "You have taught me," George II had told him, "to look for the sense of my

---

[29] *Political Papers . . . Collected by the Rev. Christopher Wyvill* (York, n.d.; hereafter referred to as *Wyvill Papers*), I:xix; *Addresses, Remonstrances and Petitions to the Throne* (London, 1865), p. 18; *Cavendish's Debates*, I:525.

[30] *Cavendish's Debates*, I:367; *Parliamentary History*, XVII:149. For a hostile description of these arguments see Richard Watson, *The Principles of the Revolution Vindicated* (Cambridge, 1776).

subjects in another place than in the House of Commons."[31] The main corps of whigs however had accepted the system on which their power depended. Only with the emergence of the king as leader of that system did they fall back on the more ancient and more liberal whig creed. Driven partly by self-interest and partly by the increasingly obvious implications of the king's intervention, the Rockingham whigs refused to recognize the legitimacy of this spurious relic of whiggism, and through the speeches of their leaders they maintained the responsibility of parliament to the electorate. "What is the House of Commons for?" asked Burke in 1769. "Is it for our names, is it for our faces that we have been sent here?"[32] The people could rightly demand the examination of grievances, and would never accept the validity of the Middlesex decision. "The voice of the people," he declared in the following year, "is a voice that is to be heard; and not the votes and resolutions of the House of Commons. . . . Nothing, I tell you, can make this House respectable but one thing. You must make yourselves amiable in the eyes of the people."[33]

But the whigs were on dangerous ground. When Burke spoke of the people he did not imply that the majority should participate in political decisions. Twenty-seven years later, he estimated the political nation as consisting of some four hundred thousand persons; and there is no reason to believe that he was more generous in 1769.[34] But in 1769 there were signs that the unrepresented majority was finding spokesmen to demand a greater share in political life. Political thinkers were carrying to its logical conclusion the assertion of human rights in the Glorious Revolution. Joseph Priestley had begun to build a new political philosophy on the foundations of Locke and Rousseau;[35] John Wilkes was contriving to unite his own personal interests with that of civil liberty; and the birth of English radicalism was announced by the formation of the first of the societies which organized the demand for parliamentary reform, the Society of the Supporters of the Bill of Rights.

---

[31] Basil Williams, *Life of William Pitt, Earl of Chatham* (London, 1915), I:309.

[32] *Cavendish's Debates*, I:380.

[33] *Ibid.*, II:137–138.

[34] *Letters on a Regicide Peace* (1796). The passage occurs near the middle of the first Letter.

[35] *An Essay on Government* (1768).

As yet the reformers were not prepared to lay rude hands on the representative system. Their most vigorous demands were for the instruction of members, more frequent elections, and the exclusion of placemen from parliament. It is true that tentative proposals were made for an addition to the representation of counties and the disfranchisement of some rotten boroughs; but these proposals involved only a more equitable distribution of existing votes, not an increase in the electorate. They sought to restore the supposedly ancient practice of the constitution, and were not yet based on a radical philosophy of change. Even so, they were unwelcome to the whigs, whose suspicions were confirmed in the next few years by the appearance of a genuinely radical program. The future was to show that no party or group could afford to ignore this growing movement, and those who called themselves whigs would soon have to decide whether their gospel of liberalism was a book closed in 1689 or a living principle of change. For the present the Rockingham whigs agreed with the king that the existing constitution of parliament must be preserved. Upon it depended their political power and their following in the Commons. This influence could not be risked in fundamental reform. The instruction of members would break the solidarity of party. Frequent elections would put an intolerable strain on private purses. A wider electorate would destroy local control. As a recent historian has remarked, getting rid of the rotten boroughs was for them too high a price to pay for getting rid of the influence of the crown.[36] The old system was essential.

And yet it was precisely this system that the king was using. He was no Stuart tyrant. He preferred to govern as a parliamentary leader. He was beating the whigs at their own game of patronage and influence. The parliament they wanted to preserve was being discredited by the arbitrary acts of the ministry; and it was not easy to attack the ministerial majority, on behalf of the electorate, without attacking parliament itself. But the whigs had to do this. They had to fight the king without destroying the source of his power which was also theirs. They were in the position of a besieging army which could not afford to hurt the fortress it was attacking. They could not hope to preserve

---

[36] R. Sedgwick, ed., *Letters from George III to Lord Bute, 1756–66*, p. xviii.

intact the entire whig system of influence, but at least they could con-
centrate their fire upon the part which was least essential to them and
most useful to him, that is, the patronage peculiar to the crown. Since
their antagonist was the king, they could also denounce his ultimate
aims as dangerous to the constitution. They might even advocate such
a small electoral change as the disfranchisement of excise officers,
proposed by Dowdeswell in 1770, but the instant that they set foot on
the slope of electoral reform they were confronted by the danger to
their own position. Charles Fox, newly appointed to office, immediately pointed out the logical tendency of Dowdeswell's motion, which,
he said, corrected one abuse but let others alone. "Let the House
remedy the influence of peers at elections. In that influence lies the
fatal influence of the Crown. . . . Every argument applied to the cus-
tomhouse officer applies equally to the influence exercised by the
peer."[37] So the whig defense of liberty remained a negative policy
which strenuously resisted any encroachment upon existing constitutional rights but was unwilling to raise the question of positive change.
By confining the ground of opposition to the immediate issue, Burke
and the Rockingham whigs clung to an aristocratic monopoly which
cut them off from the growing force of public opinion.

The ingrained conservatism of the whigs did not redeem them from
the charge of faction. On the contrary, since they could not lead a
popular crusade, they were compelled to rally opposition around a
compact aristocratic group, and in this way to develop the concept of
organized party. For a century, systematic opposition to the king's
government had been regarded as a factious conspiracy to obtain the
spoils of office by obstructing the legitimate exercise of executive
power. "Faction Detected," "Opposition Not Faction," these were not
merely the titles of famous pamphlets of the previous generation.
They were the conventional battle cries of the parliamentary arena;
and now that the king had descended into that arena and, with his
own party, the "king's friends," was vigorously taking sides, there
was no likelihood of greater leniency to formal opposition. Moreover,
the very bitterness of the engagement led Burke to justify systematic
opposition more bluntly than was customary. As early as May, 1768,

---

[37] *Cavendish's Debates,* I:450.

when the gentler Conway had deprecated the heat of party connections, Burke answered that the country would never be well governed until those who were connected by unanimity of sentiment held the reins of power. The following year he went further. "If I see any set of men acting systematically wrong," he said, "I declare that no acts of such men ought to be supported. . . . If you support these men for a year in doing wrong acts, it is confirming their power to do wrong always, merely because they may now and then do a good act. I am connected; I glory in such connexion." Here already was the voice of the great champion of party. Nevertheless, the position of Conway was the more representative, and if one who was almost of their number could scent faction in it, the attitude of Chatham is less surprising.[38]

The whiggism of Chatham was of that old order which placed the fundamental law of the constitution beyond the reach of parliament. English liberties were for him established in Magna Carta and the Bill of Rights, and they were immutable. The privileges and the authority of parliament did not extend beyond the constitution which recognized also the mutual obligations of king and people. Such an interpretation of whiggism brought Chatham very near to those tories who had accepted the Revolution settlement, and he shared their belief in a structural national unity. The practical result was a complete lack of sympathy for the whig monopoly of government, and of the supremacy of parliament on which it rested. Chatham was willing to go at least part of the way to that reform which was the hope of the radicals and anathema to Burke. He was at the same time more tolerant of royal power, and aroused whig suspicion by his extreme deference to the king. Although he supported the policy of reducing ministerial patronage, he sometimes took up an attitude of contemptuous toleration, and was reported on one occasion to be willing, if he came into office, "not to meddle with the dirty people."[39]

The cleavage between Chatham and the Rockingham whigs was sharpest on the question of organized party. He had nothing but condemnation for the systematic use of personal connections, especially those of an aristocracy whose pretensions he scorned and whose

---

[38] *Cavendish's Debates*, I:15–16, 275–277.
[39] Horace Walpole, *Last Journals* (London, 1859), II:244.

abilities he despised. "Not men but measures" was his watchword. In 1766 he had joined with the king to achieve their common ideal of a nonpartisan ministry, and he never tired of proclaiming his personal independence, free from any partisan connection. Nothing less than a united nation and a united empire would suffice as the stage for the great statesman who was also a great actor. For Chatham was supremely confident in his own opinion, and could hardly coöperate for long with those who would not submit. According to Burke, he "expected a very blind submission . . . without considering himself as having any reciprocal obligation";[40] and there is a constant note of hostility in the allusions made to Chatham by the whigs. To Newcastle he was "mad and drunk with his absolute, unlimited power and influence in the closet"; to Portland he was a "true son of Belial," whose incapacity equaled his insolence. Dowdeswell referred to his "folly," and Horace Walpole to his "haughtiness and absurdity"; Burke definitely classed him as an asset to the ministry, and hoped at most to prevent his doing much mischief.[41] It is true that common opposition often led to the use of the same arguments and the same line of attack upon the North ministry; but there was a real divergence of policy and interests separating the two groups, and the whigs must have been only too conscious that Chatham's consistent constitutional theory afforded little security for an aristocratic monopoly of power.

These were the circumstances in which the whigs launched their campaign against the ministry in 1769, and that campaign established their policy for the next thirteen years. They were compelled to join Chatham and the radicals in upholding the liberties of the electorate against an extension of parliamentary authority by ministers dependent on the king. Those ministers had disregarded civil and political rights, and there was ample ground for raising the traditional whig standard; but the ground was Chatham's and required careful watching. The Rockingham whigs needed all possible support for their crusade against the crown, but this support must come from others far different in outlook and in ultimate aim. Their own corps was gradually welded into a coherent connection, but this very fact alien-

---

[40] *Correspondence*, II:276.
[41] Turberville, *op. cit.*, II:90–96; Dowdeswell MSS (Aug. 14, 1768); Walpole, *Last Journals*, I:447; *Correspondence of Edmund Burke*, II:63–64.

ated Chatham, and personal jealousies widened the rift. The pride of
the whigs kept pace with their development as a party and hindered
their association with other leaders. As Burke commented to Rockingham, it required some delicacy to keep the lead in opposition, and
get the credit for it, without antagonizing a powerful personality like
Grenville, with whom they were agreed on the immediate issue.[42] The
radicals were still less congenial, and the whig attitude to them was
well expressed by Bishop Watson when he wrote that he detested
mobs, "thinking senseless popularity beneath the notice of genuine
Whiggism . . . but, though I disliked Mr Wilkes' mobs, I did not dislike his cause, judging that the constitution was violated in the treatment he received both from the King's ministers, and the House of
Commons."[43] Thus the whig problem was to keep temporary allies
without surrendering permanent principles.

Dowdeswell led the movement for union. In May, 1769, he invited
the minority, thrown together in the opposition lobby, to meet in the
traditional way for dinner at the Thatched House Tavern. About
seventy-two members attended, less than half the normal opposition,
but representing the followers of Rockingham, Chatham, and Grenville. The numerous toasts included the Right of Electors, the Freeholders of Middlesex, the City of London, and "Mr Henry Cavendish's
Creed" abjuring "the damnable doctrine that a resolution of the
House of Commons can make, alter, suspend, abrogate or annihilate
the Law of the Land."[44] Another meeting was arranged for the day
preceding the next parliamentary session, and for a time it seemed as
if the thread of union would hold. But as the petitions came in from
the counties it soon appeared that differences of degree were so great
that the wisest statesmanship would be needed to hold them together,
and Rockingham consulted earnestly with his friends.

The whigs were fighting the crown, and yet on this immediate question they were petitioning the crown against the House of Commons.
They recognized the paradox, and attempted to restrict petitions to
the request for dissolution. Burke and Dowdeswell insisted also that

---

[42] *Correspondence*, I:171.
[43] *Anecdotes of the Life of Richard Watson* (London, 1817), p. 34.
[44] Historical MSS Commission, 12th Rept., App. X (Charlemont MSS), p. 294; *Cavendish's Debates*, I:433–434 n.

all petitions should keep to the point of the rights of electors, and not wander into projects of reform.[45]

One of the first opportunities for whig policy to assert itself was in the petition from the County of Worcester. On August 9 a meeting was held, and, under Dowdeswell's supervision, it "kept in the distinction between the virtues of the king and the vices of the administration, and imputed the ill conduct of the H. of C. to the bad practices of the latter."[46] There was a lack of enthusiasm, however, and the petition gained signatures but slowly. People of rank and position shrank from leadership; others waited in deference. The reason, according to Dowdeswell, was a widespread dislike of Wilkes's character and opinions, fortified by the radicalism and violence shown in some early petitions.

The Yorkshire meeting followed that of Worcester. Here the local influence of the whig magnates gave a special significance to the proceedings; but there was great confusion. The meeting hesitated between instructing its members and petitioning the crown. Dowdeswell urged Rockingham to stand firm for petitions to dissolve parliament. Like Burke he saw the difficulties of instruction, and especially the room for conflict between the claims of party and those of constituents. The fear of sudden dissolution seemed to him the most effective way of arresting the progress of an arbitrary majority. Hence, with Savile, he insisted on holding strictly to this request. He recognized the danger of tampering with the settled procedure of tradition, and in particular of petitioning the crown against the House of Commons. But, he said, "unless we take parliaments as they are in fact, and not as they are on paper, we shall never be a match for our adversaries."[47]

The policy of the Yorkshire meeting was the subject of long and careful planning among the leaders of the Rockingham group. Burke, Savile, and Dowdeswell were the three persons on whom Rockingham chiefly relied, and fortunately they thought much alike. All were concerned to avoid any openings for criticism on the ground of radicalism or faction, and to keep to established constitutional practice, in spite of the novelty of the problem. They approved Rocking-

---

[45] Albemarle, *op. cit.*, II:133–134; Dowdeswell MSS.
[46] Dowdeswell MSS; Winstanley, *Lord Chatham and the Whig Opposition*, p. 278.
[47] Dowdeswell MSS (Sept. 5, 1769).

ham's decision not to attend the meeting, lest his presence should raise the partisan issue, and they made changes in the proposed petition so as to insure both constitutionality and vigor.[48]

The cautious conservatism of whig policy was more successful in guiding the popular movement in the counties than in a great urban constituency. London had already shown its radical tendencies, and in Bristol the situation was significant enough to merit special attention. Bristol politics had shared the general confusion of the 'sixties.[49] Some years earlier, the two rival organizations, whig and tory, had come to an amicable understanding, as in many other places, to spare themselves unnecessary expense in contested elections. By a gentleman's agreement, one whig and one tory member were to be supported in three successive parliaments. But with the new reign the whig member, Robert Nugent, later Lord Clare, had turned placeman and ceased to represent the interests which the whigs had chosen him to guard, especially after the American controversy began to damage Bristol trade. The merchants grew more and more dissatisfied. In 1769, following the example of London, a large gathering of whigs in Bristol, headed by Joseph Harford and Richard Champion, demanded that their members of parliament should accept instruction from their constituents, and vote accordingly. Their demands were sent to the members, but were evaded by Lord Clare. Although at first the method of instruction seemed a promising means of counteracting the influence of the crown, the whigs were soon forced to choose between a radical and a conservative position. Some of them showed their temperamental affinity with the Rockingham group, and lamented the appearance of radical leaders. "With a great and formidable appearance," wrote Champion in December, "and a real strength, the leaders are in themselves so little adequate to the task they have assumed, and conduct themselves with such a wildness of popularity, and so little attention to common sense, that with respect to the great point in view, the removal of the dangerous faction at court, which threatens destruction to the liberties of the whole empire, it can have

---

[48] Dowdeswell MSS (Sept. 5, 20); Albemarle, *op. cit.*, II:104, 132–136.
[49] Ernest Barker, *Burke and Bristol* (Bristol, n.d.); G. E. Weare, *Edmund Burke's Connection with Bristol* (Bristol, 1894); G. H. Guttridge, *The American Correspondence of a Bristol Merchant*, Univ. Calif. Publ. Hist., XXII (1934):1–72.

no effect. I engaged with the warmest and best views, and threw in my mite with the fullest intentions to contribute to the public service; but I found, to my great mortification, that the followers of Mr. Wilkes, however laudable the cause of the man, have, no more than himself, the smallest spark of patriotism about them."[50]

Thus, when the demand for the instruction of members was followed up by a petition asking also for annual parliaments, the exclusion of placemen and pensioners, and drastic changes in the representation of counties and boroughs, Champion and his friends refused to sponsor it, declaring that the radical demands it contained would discredit the cause of moderate reform and throw weight into the hands of ministers. They refused also to support the proposal for an association to advance the program of reform. "Our party," he said, "with the honest of the other, have a vast strength, and want only sensible and good men to lead them, to be made invincible. The friends of Mr. Wilkes took the advantage of the times to head them, which . . . has frightened away many very worthy men of the best principles, whose moderation is alarmed by their violence, and whose minds, naturally timid from a confined education and want of knowledge of the world, are rendered not only more irresolute, but are filled with aversion to a public appearance, tho' they wish well to it in private."[51]

This division among the whigs of Bristol, reflecting the national division of whig and radical, had important consequences. Henry Cruger and his friends stepped into the places vacated by Champion and Harford; and the sequel came in the election of 1774, when the friends of Burke could make little headway against the jealousy of the more powerful friends of Cruger, although this time they succeeded in winning the second place.

Meanwhile the petitions of 1769 were ignored by the crown, and as no organization had been formed to follow up their demands, the only hope of success lay in parliament. There the crucial question was whether the union of opposition would hold long enough to turn out the discredited ministry. Dowdeswell again applied himself to the

---

[50] MS letter books of Richard Champion. See Guttridge, *op. cit.,* and Hugh Owen, *Two Centuries of Ceramic Art in Bristol* (London, 1873), p. 59.

[51] MS letter books; Owen, *op. cit.,* p. 60.

task of insuring this union. Their potential allies, he believed, were anxious to go farther than the more conservative petitions; but even the radical leaders were old politicians, and should be induced to rest content with the ground on which all could unite.[52] Parliament did not meet until after Christmas, but early in December Burke was becoming impatient for Rockingham's return to town. Dowdeswell added his own plea, commenting that the party would not readily assemble until they knew that their leader was at hand to give the signal. He also reminded Rockingham that the preliminary meeting at the Thatched House must be fully exploited before parliament met.[53]

Chatham, for the moment, was conciliatory. Putting aside past quarrels, he made polite allusions to the need for whig leadership and the great qualities of "Lord Rockingham's spotless friends." " 'Spotless' sounds very well," remarked Savile, "but it does not convey to me the idea of all being settled with confidence and comfortable cordiality all in a minute."[54] Nevertheless a working alliance was formed on the basis of supporting the rights of electors and of destroying the king's men "as a corps." In everything else, the new allies agreed, "we were both free to play the fool as much as we pleased."[55]

Even so, they could not beat the king. They drove Grafton from his uneasy eminence, but only to seat a more formidable opponent, Lord North. The new chief minister had the advantage of being a member of the House of Commons, and there he could meet cleverness with cleverness. Thus when Dowdeswell made two motions on the right of election which seemed almost impossible to deny, North turned the flank of the first by an amendment which made it self-contradictory; and, meeting the second squarely, defeated it by a small majority.[56] Then, when Grenville reinforced the whig attack by a proposal to end the scandal of decision by majority on disputed elections, North survived by withdrawing ministerial opposition.[57]

Defeat was averted, and the tide began to turn. The City of London,

---

[52] Dowdeswell MSS (Sept. 20, 1769).

[53] *Correspondence of Edmund Burke*, I:218; Dowdeswell MSS (Dec. 16, 1769).

[54] Albemarle, *op. cit.*, II:142.

[55] *Correspondence of Edmund Burke*, I:208–209, 216.

[56] *Parliamentary History*, XVI:785 ff.; Winstanley, *Lord Chatham and the Whig Opposition*, pp. 330–335.

[57] Winstanley, *Lord Chatham and the Whig Opposition*, pp. 349–352.

exasperated by the neglect of its petition, addressed to the king a remonstrance denouncing in violent terms the ministers, the "secret and malign influence" behind them, and the majority of the House of Commons. This was going too far, and when Lord North shrewdly brought it before parliament, even the moderate Conway declared it to be an attack not only upon one parliament, but upon parliaments in general.[58] Burke attempted to excuse the violence of the City just as he was attempting to excuse that of America; but the whigs were not happy in such company.[59] When the Yorkshire freeholders also suggested a remonstrance at their meeting in September, both Lord John Cavendish and Sir George Savile discouraged it, and the meeting took no effective action.[60] Chatham was already blaming the conservatism of Lord Rockingham's friends. "Moderation, moderation," he said, "is the burden of the song."[61] And although Burke could not conceal his satisfaction at the waning influence of "that wretched knot" of radicals, yet even he felt a wistfulness in sight of the missed opportunity. "We never shall have a matter so well calculated to engage [the people]," he wrote to Rockingham; "opposition is upon narrow and delicate ground, especially that part of opposition which acts with your lordship; you and your friends having exceedingly contracted the field of operations."[62]

Restricted and exclusive as were the aims of the party, it was necessary to justify them to the country; and the difficult task had already fallen to Burke. "This can only be done," he wrote, "by showing the ground upon which the party stands, and how different its constitution, as well as the persons who compose it are from the Bedfords and Grenvilles and other knots, who are combined for no public purpose, but only as a means of furthering with joint strength their private and individual advantage." The result was the *Thoughts on the Cause of the Present Discontents.*[63]

---

[58] *Addresses, Remonstrances and Petitions to the Throne* . . . (London, 1865), p. 18; *Cavendish's Debates,* I:534–553.

[59] *Cavendish's Debates,* I:544–545.

[60] *Wyvill Papers,* I:xxii–xxxv; Winstanley, *Lord Chatham and the Whig Opposition,* p. 364.

[61] *Correspondence of William Pitt,* III:469.

[62] *Correspondence of Edmund Burke,* I:233, 237.

[63] *Correspondence,* I:203.

This pamphlet, published in April, 1770, was begun much earlier, and the manuscript was circulated among the group for criticism. Rockingham, Portland, Dowdeswell, and Savile examined it; and Rockingham, after keeping it for several weeks, requested Burke and Dowdeswell to make a final examination of the comments. Savile, though agreeing with the ideas expressed, questioned the wisdom of publishing the pamphlet; and even Burke himself had some doubts whether they should commit themselves as completely as this declaration of policy would do. Even after some changes he pointed out that the manifesto would irritate the court past forgiveness, without conciliating other groups in opposition. Nevertheless, they all believed that the *Thoughts* would hold out a banner to young men of property and independence in parliament, and would call them, in Rockingham's words, "to form and unite a party upon real and well-founded principles."[64]

The importance of Burke's pamphlet can hardly be exaggerated, but its publication showed how well justified were his misgivings. Appearing at the very time when Lord North was leading the king's friends to a more united and triumphant course, it demolished the old division of whig and tory, and bluntly and exclusively set forth the new. "Few are the partisans of departed tyranny, and to be a whig on the business of a hundred years ago is very consistent with every advantage of present servility." The new toryism as Burke saw it—and the term was already being used—was that of the king's followers in parliament. "The power of the crown, almost dead and rotten as prerogative, has grown up anew, with much more strength and far less odium under the name of influence."[65] The king, by building a court party and maintaining a secret cabinet, was able to direct policy through ostensible ministers, and to kick away that aristocratic support which had preserved the throne since the Revolution. Aristocratic power was resented, and aristocratic connections systematically undermined. Parliament under this influence was becoming an adjunct of monarchy,

[64] Albemarle, *op. cit.*, II:144–147; *Correspondence of Edmund Burke*, I:198, 205, 218.

[65] Cf. Dowdeswell's speech in parliament on February 12, 1770: "What the Crown formerly claimed by Prerogative it now claims by virtue of Influence," etc.—*Cavendish's Debates*, I:443.

acquiescing in the royal schemes and virtually granting an unlimited revenue by paying the king's debts. By appropriating the power of declaring incapacity in elections, it was exercising for the crown an arbitrary jurisdiction comparable only to that of the Star Chamber.

Against this design Burke appealed to "the natural strength of the kingdom, the great peers, the leading landed gentlemen, the opulent merchants and manufacturers, the substantial yeomanry," who "must interpose to rescue their prince, themselves and their posterity." In that enterprise they must use the resources of party, the firm association in parliament of a group whose function he now defined in memorable words. "Party," he wrote, "is a body of men united, for promoting by their joint endeavours the national interest, upon some particular principle, in which they are all agreed." But parliamentary resistance was not enough. "Until a confidence in government is re-established, the people ought to be excited to a more strict and detailed attention to the conduct of their representatives. Standards for judging more systematically upon their conduct ought to be settled in the meetings of counties and corporations. Frequent and correct lists of the voters in all important questions ought to be procured." In other words, the whig program here outlined was a program of resistance to the king by a parliamentary opposition united as a party under aristocratic leadership and supported by the existing narrow electorate of property.

In laying down these principles of government Burke made clear the gulf which separated his own party from the "detached gentlemen" like Chatham, and also from the radicals. The exclusion of placemen from parliament seemed to him a dangerous blow to efficient government, and a threat of extraparliamentary organization. Frequent elections would assist the crown by "committing the independent gentlemen of the country into a contest with the treasury"; and an enlargement of the franchise he did not even consider, tempted though all leaders of opposition are to look for support outside the existing political arena. The aristocracy whose cause he upheld had their special mandate from the people, and that must suffice.

This program inevitably failed to satisfy the radicals and was criticized unsparingly by them. Radical opposition to the king was based largely on arguments which applied with equal force to the continued

rule of the whig aristocrats, "who, by their long possession and constant disposal of all offices, both civil and military, think they have
acquired an indefeasible, if not a hereditary right to the continuance
of themselves and friends in their respective employs."[66] "The state
reformers at the Revolution," wrote one pamphleteer, "were so intent
on binding down our kings to their good behaviour, that they left the
grandees in possession of powers inconsistent with the first principles
of liberty."[67]

The radicals were not slow in replying to Burke's manifesto. Catherine Macaulay, who was never afraid of speaking her mind, undertook
what she called the "invidious task of making disagreeable observations upon [its] baneful tendency."[68] Her blunt and abusive *Observations* are the more illuminating for their brevity and simplicity. Her
creed was not deeply philosophical. In some degree it revived the
a priori reasoning which had already been outmoded by the work of
Montesquieu, Hume, and Burke. Nevertheless it contained an ele-
mentary assertion of liberty and the needs of the majority, which was
a necessary supplement to Burke. Believing that "to plan a form of
government perfect in its nature and consequently answering all its
just ends is neither morally impossible in itself nor beyond the abilities of man," Catherine Macaulay saw in the force of custom, not the
beneficent process beloved by Burke, but merely the propensity which
"has ever afforded full opportunity to the interested to reject every
part of reformation which tends effectually to establish public good
on the ruins of private interest."[69] Burke's manifesto endeavored, she
said, under the guise of attacking the dangerous designs of the crown,
to mislead the people on the no less dangerous maneuvers of aristocratic faction and party, based on the self-interest of "a misinformed
and selfish nobility," who had made parliament their instrument, and
had turned the nation into the creditors instead of the paymasters of
government. Septennial parliaments and high taxation had enriched
the few, whose main grievance against the king was that he had de-

---

[66] William Guthrie, *An Address to the Public* (1764), printed in *A Collection of
Scarce and Interesting Tracts* (London, 1788), I:348.
[67] *Political Register* (1768), p. 222.
[68] *Observations on . . . Thoughts on the Cause of the Present Discontents* (London,
1770), p. 5.
[69] *Ibid.*, p. 9.

prived them of their rewards. "Disappointed ambition has led them to offer their services to an alarmed and enraged populace"; but it was now necessary to go further and destroy, by a thoroughgoing reform, the lucrative advantages of membership in parliament. Burke's objection to the expense of frequent elections would then fall to the ground.[70]

To Chatham also Burke's pamphlet was displeasing for its attack on the nonpartisan position—"the cant of 'not men but measures' "— and its insistence on the supreme merit of party. Burke declared long afterward that his pamphlet was an answer by anticipation to Chatham, "that grand artificer of fraud." A few months after its publication Chatham wrote to Rockingham that it had done much harm to the cause. "Allow me, my lord . . . to press again and again large and comprehensive views. . . . The *whole* alone can save the *whole* against the desperate designs of the court."[71]

The sequel soon came. In the following year the freedom of the press was threatened by a decision of Lord Mansfield that juries in cases of libel could not decide the vital question whether the matter complained of was libelous or not. This was an issue on which widespread support might be rallied in parliament and outside. The opposition agreed that the practice must be changed; but basic differences of constitutional interpretation prevailed when methods were discussed. Chatham believed that Lord Mansfield's judgment violated fundamental rights. He therefore sought to convict him of error by a declaratory act upholding the constitution. The duty of parliament, as he saw it, was to declare the law. Dowdeswell, for the Rockingham whigs, agreed that civil and political liberties were threatened; but for him the remedy lay in the supreme authority of parliament to change the law. Legislation, not interpretation, was the function of parliament, and he introduced a bill to this end. Personal jealousies and partisan suspicions embittered the disagreement. Justifying their action by the need of satisfying the lawyers, Burke and Rockingham determined to stand fast with Dowdeswell. The aim of Chatham, said Burke, was to prevent the other group from any useful achievement. Chatham, said Rockingham, was carried away by animosity toward

[70] *Ibid.*, pp. 5, 6, 11.
[71] Albemarle, *op. cit.*, II:193–195.

Mansfield and jealousy of themselves, and must not be suffered to wreck the plan of reform. Dowdeswell listened to these arguments, and consulted other whig leaders. The result was merely to strengthen his own determination to persist.[72]

So the final outcome of the long-awaited whig attack was a miserable fiasco. Dowdeswell's obstinacy was, to Chatham, "a compound of connection, tyranny and absurdity," a proof of the "spirit of connection," a sign that everything not stamped with the name of Rockingham was disapproved of, and—a parting shot for Dowdeswell—another sign of the "reign of dullness in opposition."[73] Rockingham, with all the tact of what Chatham himself called his candid and temperate manner,[74] could not close the rift; and the opposition was defeated, no longer by a small majority, but in a rout which proved decisive. The principle of party had been maintained, and the cause had been lost.

In 1772 and 1773 the whigs reached the nadir of their fortunes. Cooperation between Rockingham and Chatham had failed. "The narrow genius of old-corps' connection," wrote Chatham, "has weakened Whiggism, and rendered national union on revolution principles impossible." Shelburne lamented the "secret influence," which seemed to have crept into opposition;[75] and the ministry could contemplate the confusion of a once united front. The House of Commons was tired of the Middlesex election and the rights of electors. Whig attempts to revive the topic aroused only the increasing impatience of the majority.

Moreover, the questions which arose to concern the whigs most nearly were peculiarly unsatisfactory for a great crusade. The Royal Marriage Bill could be opposed on the ground that it enlarged the prerogative by requiring the king's consent to marriages within the royal family, but it was too trivial for an appeal to the nation. Proposals to relieve dissenters and moderate churchmen of subscription to the Thirty-nine Articles won few recruits to the whig cause, and

[72] *Correspondence of Edmund Burke*, I:251; Albemarle, *op. cit.*, II:200–204; Dowdeswell MSS (Feb. 2, 16, 1771).
[73] *Correspondence of William Pitt*, IV:100–104.
[74] *Ibid.*, p. 108.
[75] *Ibid.*, pp. 187, 189.

were not even wholly acceptable to the main corps. The Duke of Portland's long struggle for the possession of lands to which he lacked title rallied aristocratic supporters but not the public at large. The complicated problems of the East India Company distressed them by divisions, or at best united them in defense of unpopular vested interests. And when parliament took up the attempt of Ireland to tax absentee landowners, the whigs were touched by a direct attack on their own wealth. The more liberal could see some justice in the proposal; but the majority were carried away by the violation of the sacred rights of property, or by the attempt to prevent the residence of landowners in the metropolis of the empire.[76]

The whigs were short of ammunition, and disputed among themselves. They looked in vain for a great cause in which they could revive the agitation of 1769. Lord North was a warier minister than Grafton; and until America became the first political topic, the great cause was lacking. In these circumstances it was only natural that many of the whig leaders, who were in no sense professional politicians, should advocate a policy of abstention or secession from parliament. Immediately after the break with Chatham the drift was clear. A contest had begun between the City of London and the House of Commons over the printing of parliamentary debates, but in spite of the apparent opportunity for a concerted attack in the manner of 1769, Rockingham and Dowdeswell both expressed their determination to stay away and leave the ministry unchecked, lest by ineffective comment they should assist rather than retard.[77] Sir George Savile and the two Burkes walked out of the House while the debate was on.[78] Others continued the parliamentary struggle; but the only policy on which all agreed was that of paying a formal and solemn visit in a body to the Lord Mayor imprisoned in the Tower.

From this time the movement to secede from parliament gained ground. In May the Duke of Richmond described politics as at a standstill and announced his preference for a return to country life until the accumulated misconduct of administration should create an-

---

[76] Dowdeswell MSS (Nov. 26, 1773); Albemarle, *op. cit.*, II:226–234; *Correspondence of Edmund Burke*, I:440–441.

[77] Dowdeswell MSS (Mar. 28, 1771); Albemarle, *op. cit.*, II:210.

[78] *Cavendish's Debates*, II:461, 472, 475.

other crisis in the country. "So many subdivisions of the weakest party, the opposition," he wrote, "can never overturn the great majority which the influence of the crown gives to court."[79] A year later, in May, 1772, there was serious disagreement on the same matter of policy. Sir George Savile still maintained that the opposition could and should attend to criticize the measures of the ministry.[80] Dowdeswell, who until the previous year had been energetic in pursuing his parliamentary duty, announced his intention of staying in the country and attending to his private affairs. "I am inclined to leave business now to Lord North," he told Burke.[81] He was anxious, however, to avert a possible break which might send Savile and his friends out of the party, and the two sections met to preserve a common policy. The parliamentary vacation gave more time for consideration, but when the new session approached in October, Dowdeswell was still despondent. "In every place except the City," he wrote to Rockingham, "men are deaf to every call which should awake them. Where they are awake they are too lively, and run to every trumpet. In such a time I think one's chimney corner the pleasantest place."[82] Rockingham, Keppel, Richmond, and Burke all expressed their agreement with a concerted plan of secession, although Burke declared himself willing to join in a policy of activity if Rockingham and Dowdeswell agreed upon it. They were, he believed, morally sure of being defeated, and could only hope to save their honor.[83]

The decision had soon to be made. From his chimney corner in Worcestershire Dowdeswell was active in composing plans of campaign for the group to discuss. He made elaborate preparations for action on the pending affairs of the East India Company, but still felt that complete abstention from attendance at Westminster was the best course, at least for the first two weeks of the session. Agreeing with Savile that such action could be justified only at times of fundamental constitutional crisis, Dowdeswell believed that the crisis existed. "The system long in practice," he wrote, "the fruitless opposition

---

[79] Dowdeswell MSS (May 20, 1771).
[80] Albemarle, *op. cit.*, II:225–226.
[81] Dowdeswell MSS (May 5, 1772).
[82] Dowdeswell MSS (Oct. 18, 1772).
[83] *Correspondence of Edmund Burke*, I:346–348.

we have made, the treachery of false brethren, and the disposition of the public to give credit to the imputation of private designs ... bring us in despair to let the public see itself in the hands of government, and at least free ourselves from all unnecessary trouble and if possible from the imputation of fretful opposition and selfish design."[84]

Burke, however, although originally favorable to the plan, found that many of Rockingham's friends disagreed. He therefore advised against it, on the ground that unanimity was essential to its success.[85] The others reluctantly agreed, but saw no need to be prompt in their attendance in London. Dowdeswell wrote that private affairs would make him a few days late, and urged Rockingham to put the restoration of his own health before a hurried journey to town.[86] Richmond protested against the hasty summons, and saw little hope for the party. "You say," he wrote to Burke, "the party is an object of too much importance to be let go to pieces. Indeed, Burke, you have more merit than any man in keeping us together; but I believe our greatest bond is the pride of the individuals, which, unfortunately, though it keeps us from breaking, hinders us from acting like men of sense. The marquis manages us better than any man can, but he will never make us what we ought to be; the thing is not practicable."[87]

It was soon necessary to appeal to Rockingham's gift of management. In January, 1773, in a debate on East Indian affairs, Lord George Sackville Germain took occasion to differ strongly from the Rockingham whigs. Germain, whose ignominy after the battle of Minden was to be equaled only by the discredit he acquired as secretary of state for the American colonies during the war, was for a short time a prominent, if not influential, member of the Rockingham whigs. Under their administration he had been restored to public life in 1765, to the disgust of Chatham; and in 1772 he had apparently come to regard himself as destined for whig leadership in the House of Commons. Burke and his friends, however, could not accept this ambition. Moreover, Dowdeswell possessed far too firm a hold on the respect and affection of the group to be ousted by so questionable a leader as

---

[84] Dowdeswell MSS (Nov. 3, 8, 1772); *Correspondence of Edmund Burke,* I:356.
[85] *Correspondence,* I:365–369.
[86] Dowdeswell MSS (Nov. 19, 1772).
[87] *Correspondence of Edmund Burke,* I:371.

Germain.[88] Burke therefore urged his leader to come and restore order. "We fall into confusion the moment you turn your back," he declared. "Nobody but yourself has the means of rightly managing the different characters, and reconciling the different interests, that make up the corps of opposition. . . . My great uneasiness is about our own corps, which appears to me in great danger of dissolution. Nothing can prevent it in my opinion but the speedy and careful application of your lordship's own peculiar, persuasive and conciliatory manner."[89]

The defection of Lord George Germain was followed by that of Charles Wolfran Cornwall, and the remnant of the party had to console itself for loss of numbers by gain in principle. "Our indifference to the emoluments of office," wrote Dowdeswell, "except when they may be accompanied also by the honours of it, our steady and temperate adherence to our own principles whether in place or in opposition, do not suit gentlemen who, anxious for the profits of office, and indifferent to the means of obtaining them, run into every measure that may raise clamour, excite public expectation without the least intention of gratifying it, and hold out their hands more than half way to the court, ready to engage with any minister, and to support any measure."[90]

This was the state of the group when the Boston tea party led to measures of punishment and coercion against the colonies, and eventually gave the whigs the cause for which they had been waiting and on which they could unite. "Your lordship," Burke told Rockingham in February, 1774, "will find all your friends, though not active, yet all at their posts; in good humour with one another, in no bad spirits; firmly attached to their principles and to your lordship."[91]

It would be an impossible task to draw up a precise list of a party which did not exist as a well-defined body. Any attempt to indicate a thoroughly coherent group would reduce the number to a point obviously out of relation to the political importance of the party, and

---

[88] *Correspondence of Edmund Burke,* I:407–415; G. H. Guttridge, "Lord George Germain in Office, 1775–82," *Am. Hist. Rev.,* XXXIII (Oct., 1927):23–43.
[89] *Correspondence,* I:417, 422.
[90] Dowdeswell MSS (July 18, 1773).
[91] *Correspondence,* I:451.

the inclusion of all who were in some degree of political contact with one another would produce a meaningless procession the tail of which might be found in the ministerial camp. It is especially difficult to draw any satisfactory line between those who followed Rockingham and those who supported Chatham; for Chatham's reiteration of his nonpartisan and unconnected position attracted many whigs and at the same time made it unnecessary for them to profess formal allegiance. It cannot be too often recalled that the habit of independence was ingrained among a large number of members of parliament, and that Burke's justification of systematic party was strange and new. There were probably few of Rockingham's own friends who accepted its full implications, to the point of repudiating their freedom of choice. Only the most prominent were obliged to admit their connection, and even they had frequent qualms. The habit of association is, however, an important factor in the history of party, and the Rockingham whigs formed that habit effectively during the long ministry of Lord North. It is therefore practicable to indicate those who were normally the leaders in framing policy or at least in criticizing it. These leaders may be divided, again only approximately, into several groups.

First, apart from Rockingham himself, the only marquis in the House of Lords, came the dukes and other important peers, who used their vast social and territorial influence for the whig cause, and who in return possessed a presumptive right to consultation and ultimately to high ministerial office. Among the Rockingham whigs in the 'seventies this group would include the Dukes of Devonshire, Portland, Manchester, and Richmond, Earl Fitzwilliam and the Earl of Effingham. Of these, Manchester and Fitzwilliam represented the more conservative right wing, while Richmond stood at the extreme left nearest to Chatham, with Effingham not far away. The Duke of Devonshire, head of the Cavendishes, was himself a young and silent peer, emerging in politics only toward the end of the war, but his uncles, especially Lord John Cavendish, upheld the parliamentary reputation and influence of the family, always on the conservative side. The Duke of Portland, closely related to the Cavendishes, was throughout one of the most respected leaders, and a firm adherent to the principle of party as a coherent group of men who thought alike. He had already in 1766 referred to himself as "a servant of the party," and to that position he clung as faithfully as Burke. "I . . . have always acted with a party," he declared in 1780; and in the previous year this "very wise and very good man" remarked to Burke that he never knew any man to disclaim party who was not of a party that he was ashamed of.[92] It was this devoted service, rather than conspicuous ability, which later raised Portland to the highest office in the state. Of the other peers Manchester, Richmond, Fitzwilliam, and Effingham were all active in debate, although as a class they had small inclination for the arduous efforts of maintaining a party in difficult times.

Next in social significance came the influential commoners, headed by the unique figure of Sir George Savile. Savile was a landowner with great estates in Yorkshire and Nottinghamshire, and represented the former county in the House of Commons from 1759 to 1783. His great reputation among his contemporaries sprang from a combination of influence, ability, and integrity. He was above suspicion in matters of interest, performed many important parliamentary duties, and came to be regarded as the perfect example of a county member. Nor was his public virtue without distinctive color. He was an able speaker and enriched his conversation and his correspondence with a wealth of pithy and vigorous phrase. He was not bound at all costs to the party, nor to the doctrine of complete parliamentary supremacy, upon which the principle of party rested. He had no desire for office, and preferred the role of senator in the sense which still survived in the eighteenth century, that is, the member of a legislative body which existed in its own right, and which, in the last resort, was independent of crown, ministry, and "mobility." This principle of political conduct brought Savile very near to Chatham's insistence on "measures, not men"; and although he usually acted with Rockingham and Burke, they risked losing his support if they failed to meet his high standards of parliamentary conduct.

Less wealthy, but in the same class of proud and influential country gentlemen and knights of the shire, stood William Dowdeswell. Ap-

---

[92] Turberville, *op. cit.*, II:92; Albemarle, *op. cit.*, II:411; *Correspondence of Edmund Burke*, II:277.

pearing in the inner councils of the whigs only with his appointment to high office in 1765, he threw himself vigorously into building and defending the party, and his death in 1775 deprived the whigs of their most active leader apart from Burke. The social stratum which included Dowdeswell also contained such members of parliament as Conway, Fox, Thomas Townshend, and Admiral Keppel; but of these Conway had been long a minister of the crown and was suspicious of organized opposition, while Fox, a new recruit in 1775, was never wholly assimilated. As a class they were eligible for high office.

Below the country gentlemen of independent social and political influence, and rarely rising to cabinet rank, were men like Edmund Burke, George Byng, and David Hartley. They were the workers of the party. Men of higher status might devote much time to politics. Savile, Dowdeswell, and even the Duke of Richmond were no idlers. But with them the routine of party was performed as of grace; with Burke it was a duty. As Rockingham's "man of business" he was often the inspiration of the group, but always its drudge. His ability in holding the party together was exceeded only by his power of political thought and expression; and though ultimately his great talents brought him to the threshold of high office, he never achieved it. Even his leadership of the party in the Commons might be regarded as a social error. It may be that the ultimate barrier which kept Burke in a subordinate position was not aristocratic prejudice, but the recognition that his great gifts were accompanied by a lack of balance in speech and action, which unfitted him for power.[93] Whatever the reason, he accepted his exclusion.

As Burke was the protégé of Rockingham, and Byng of Portland, so Hartley, the most single-minded opponent of the American war, owed his prominence to Sir George Savile.[94] In the struggles of the 'sixties he had devoted his talents in finance to the service of his patron's cause as a pamphleteer. Like Burke at Bristol, Hartley gained a seat in parliament for a large constituency, Hull, at the election of 1774, and by his activity rose to be ultimately independent of a patron.

---

[93] Barker, *op. cit.*, pp. 60–61; Sir Philip Magnus, *Edmund Burke* (London, 1939), p. 56.

[94] G. H. Guttridge, *David Hartley, M.P., an Advocate of Conciliation, 1774–1783,* Univ. Calif. Publ. Hist., XIV (1926):231–340.

Moreover, though the son of a physician who was more famous as a philosopher, Hartley had some pretensions to the class of country gentleman; and his half brother was member for the county of Berkshire. Here, in fact, is an example of how the party might be built up. Colonel W. H. Hartley, an independent county member, admittedly followed the lead of his elder brother, David, who was in turn a follower of Sir George Savile. The association of Savile with Rockingham thus automatically brought three parliamentary votes from this connection alone.

The class of working or professional members included such few lawyers as the party contained. In marked contrast to the little group led first by Chatham and later by Shelburne, Rockingham's friends included few distinguished lawyers. John Lee, who occupied several legal posts before becoming attorney general in 1783, was the most prominent, and may be regarded as a leader regularly consulted by Rockingham and Burke.

In the church also the Rockingham whigs counted few notable adherents. Royal patronage was nowhere more effective than in the higher ecclesiastical appointments. During the first ten years of the new reign, some of the bishops continued to vote with opposition; but their numbers dwindled. In 1763 nine were willing to support Newcastle on the cider tax; in 1767 there were seven in the minority; but by the outbreak of the American war the opposition could count only on two.[95] These two bishops, Hinchliffe of Peterborough and Shipley of St. Asaph, were not directly connected with Rockingham, and may rather be numbered as adherents of Chatham. It was hardly to be expected, however, that the bishops should play an active part in partisan leadership, and their affiliations were either ministerial or whig in the broadest sense. One of the most vigorous ecclesiastical opponents of the American war was Richard Watson, regius professor of divinity at Cambridge. He was a great admirer of Sir George Savile, and may be classified in the same semi-independent category of friendship with Rockingham, whom he addressed as "the head of the whig interest in this kingdom," and with whom he concerted measures to

---

[95] Norman Sykes, *Church and State in England in the XVIIIth Century* (Cambridge, 1934), pp. 51–52. A third, Law of Carlisle, should perhaps be added.

prevent "the Whig University of Cambridge being called upon to play the second fiddle to the Tory University of Oxford."[96]

It is a well-known fact that during the American Revolution many high officers in the army and the navy were politically in sympathy with the opposition. The extent to which this operated to damp the energy of military and naval operations is an interesting and speculative question beyond the scope of the present purpose. Actual leadership in organized opposition is a different matter. So far as a line may be drawn between Rockingham and Chatham, it would seem that the latter possessed greater influence among whig admirals and generals. Many of them had shared his triumph in the Seven Years' War, and they tended with him to profess themselves independent of party. But among the high officers who were also members of great landed families, a few may be regarded as sharing the confidence of Rockingham and Burke. General Conway was in a peculiar position. His authority was great in all matters relating to conciliation with America, and after the beginning of hostilities he was close to Rockingham. For several years previously, however, he had been reluctant to commit himself to party, and had served under Chatham. Admiral Keppel was a more consistent supporter of the political group. Like his fellow admiral, Sir Charles Saunders, who died in 1775, he had sat at the Board of Admiralty during the short Rockingham administration. He had early resigned from Chatham's ministry, and he remained an intimate adviser of Rockingham, especially, though not exclusively, on naval affairs. The climax came in 1778 and 1779, when his inconclusive engagement with the French fleet became the occasion of a violent partisan controversy, the most extreme example of the introduction of politics into the execution of the war.[97]

The commercial allies of Rockingham occupied a special place, aside from the whig hierarchy but often influential in its councils. At the time of the repeal of the Stamp Act, merchants like Trecothick and Sir William Baker were in the innermost circles of whig policy. By the next decade they were less prominent. Many merchants had been carried beyond the conservative reforms of Rockingham, and

[96] *Anecdotes of the Life of Richard Watson*, pp. 55, 57.
[97] See below, p. 108.

were demanding the instruction of members or radical changes in representation; while others accepted the coercion of America as an inevitable method of enforcing their mercantile claims. William Baker the younger was rejected for the city of London in 1774 when he refused to accept the principle of instruction of members by their constituents.[98] He found a seat in 1777, but only for a borough in the Rockingham interest. Representing a point of view different from that of the landowners and country gentlemen, he exerted some influence on whig policy after that time.

Another important link with the merchants was the friendship of Burke and Richard Champion of Bristol.[99] Champion was largely responsible for Burke's election for that city in 1774; and there he upheld the banner of the Rockingham whigs, like Baker in London, when many of his fellows had passed to the more radical policy represented by Cruger. Only with difficulty was Burke's candidacy achieved; his success was due partly to accident; and he was never reëlected. For six critical years, however, he was member for Bristol; and close ties of friendship made Champion a regular correspondent and source of information for the whig leaders. In 1775 and 1776 he was sending them the latest news from Bristol and from America, and, judging by the cordial tone of the acknowledgments, there can be no doubt that these "frequent and authentic" communications were regarded as important. Champion's relations with Burke were by this time on a plane of friendship and intimacy which makes their letters a well-defined and voluminous section of Burke's correspondence. In them can be found the details of those many concerns which they shared during the years of war. It was to Champion that Burke wrote to ascertain the effect of a speech on the electors of Bristol, to suggest the reprinting of effective opposition pieces in the Bristol papers, and to assist the subscription for American prisoners of war. Burke and Champion took counsel together on their political strategy in procuring petitions from the electors, or in opposing petitions from the ministerial group. The political confusion in Bristol survived the

[98] D. M. Clark, *British Opinion and the American Revolution* (New Haven, 1930), p. 166.

[99] See works cited above, pp. 38 and 39; also Dixon Wecter, *Edmund Burke and His Kinsmen* (Boulder, Colorado, 1939).

election of 1774, and Burke's friends retained their own caucus, meeting usually at the Bell Tavern to drink fervent whig toasts.[100]

In the absence of formal organization, different members of the party were consulted on different occasions. Before 1774 Rockingham was likely to seek the advice of Dowdeswell, Burke, Portland, and Savile; but during the summer months the accident of neighborhood tended to create a "northern conciliabulum" of Portland, Savile, and the Cavendishes; while Burke, Dowdeswell, and Richmond were far away in the south and west. After Dowdeswell's death in 1775, Burke was foremost in handling affairs peculiar to the House of Commons, with due regard to Lord John Cavendish, Frederic Montagu, Thomas Townshend, and John Lee. By this time also Charles Fox was acquiring great influence as a parliamentarian and was in close touch with Rockingham's friends. William Baker was in frequent communication with Burke, especially after 1777 and in regard to commercial matters. Naval affairs were the province of Admiral Keppel, whose intimacy with Rockingham gave him great partisan significance. On occasions when social and territorial influence was more important, as in the visit to the imprisoned lord mayor in 1771 or the procession supporting Keppel in 1779, and in matters relating to proceedings in the House of Lords, the prominent figures would be Portland, Manchester, Fitzwilliam, Richmond, and Effingham. The inner council in 1779, according to a satirical pamphlet of that date, comprised Rockingham, Richmond, Cavendish, Fox, Conway, Lee, and Townshend; with Burke, Byng, and Dr. Brocklesby in attendance "on stools," and "at the door."[101]

---

[100] In 1775 the struggle between Champion and Wedgwood, over a patent for the manufacture of hard-paste porcelain, ran on strictly partisan lines. Champion mustered the support of Rockingham, Portland, and Burke, while Wedgwood relied on Earl Gower and the Bedford Whigs. The controversy was eventually arbitrated by Rockingham and Gower.—Owen, *Two Centuries of Ceramic Art in Bristol*, pp. 113–151.

[101] [T. Tickell,] *Opposition Mornings: with Betty's Remarks* (London, 1779).

III. THE WHIGS AND AMERICA

AT PRECISELY the time when England was undergoing a revival of acute political controversy, an urgent imperial problem clamored for attention. The outline of that problem is well known. The American colonies had grown up within a system designed to increase the maritime and commercial resources of the English state, without competing unduly with existing economic interests. For a hundred years that system had remained rigid while conditions in England and in America had greatly changed. The colonies were developing into communities with economic needs that were diversified and complicated far beyond the simple conception of western plantations producing the raw materials and exotic goods needed to supplement the more advanced economy of the mother country. A persistently unfavorable balance of trade and an increasing burden of debt bore witness to the need for reorganization of commercial policy, but little was done, even at the opportunity of 1763, to correct the shortcomings of a theoretically balanced empire.

While American conditions were changing, so also were the motives of mercantile regulation. The increasing importance of parliament encouraged the appearance of powerful groups seeking to influence that regulation by political pressure. The power of such interests in parliamentary legislation justifies to some degree the epigram that mercantilism had changed from the control of trade in the interest of national policy to the control of national policy in the interest of trade. The Molasses Act is a clear example of legislation which, for the sake of the West India interest, imposed intolerable restrictions on the northern colonies, the needs of which could not be adequately supplied without considerable freedom of trade with the foreign islands. The necessity of the New England merchants broke the bands of legislation, and the act was largely evaded by smuggling. There were other reasons for evasion; there was serious friction over details, and an increasing sense of frustration. The colonies had long realized that parliament, with its powerful economic interests, was a more dangerous ruler than the king or his ministers. As early as 1731 they had become uneasy at the growing concern taken by the legislature in their affairs.[1] The trend of English constitutional development, however, could not be reversed; and when George Grenville attempted to stiffen and enforce control, the colonists began to consider the entire basis of parliamentary regulation, which had hitherto been accepted almost universally in England and very widely in America.

The peace of 1763 had not only shown the weak spots in commercial regulation. It had opened new problems of frontier settlement, trade, and defense. From the English point of view the needs of imperial policy were the provision of, and revenue to support, a broad scheme of American defense and exploitation which would include land settlement and trade regulation. As some contemporary writers realized, the whole economic basis of the empire was involved;[2] but such great conceptions rarely appeared in practical policy. The tendency of ministers was to limit their outlook to administrative and financial details, and, superficially at least, the American Revolution came about for lack of an adequate administrative and financial plan.

Such a plan might well have been invented; but time was necessary for its formulation and execution, and neither the events of America nor the politics of England withheld their claims to attention long enough for such preparation. The promising beginnings associated with the names of Halifax and Shelburne were thwarted by the pressing needs of Indian war, English finance, and colonial opposition. The result was that separate parts of a comprehensive scheme were set up to face alone the opposition which might not have wrecked the plan as a whole. Such was the Stamp Act of 1765, an attempt to obtain revenue for a policy not yet developed. Such was also the Townshend budget of 1767, to raise money without waiting for the slow progress of an American design. Both aroused colonial resistance and thus introduced in urgent form the problem of compromise or enforcement, centering around the rights of parliament. Once this basic matter of authority became controversial, the difficulties were increased tenfold.

The policy of Grenville marked the culmination of a long process

---

[1] *Calendar of State Papers, Colonial, America and West Indies*, 1731, p. xix; 1732, p. xxiv.

[2] For example: *The Present State of Great Britain and North America* (London, 1767); Thomas Pownall, *The Administration of the Colonies* (4th ed., London, 1768).

of political friction. In many of the colonies the assembly had come to demand full parliamentary status on the English model, thus raising the question of ultimate authority within the colony. The governor was often dependent upon his assembly for the means of carrying on his administration, and could rarely obtain a permanent civil list. Meanwhile in England parliament had attained virtual supremacy, and thereby assumed a relation to the colonial assemblies not unlike that of the Stuart kings to their parliaments. For long it had threatened to impose direct taxation if the assemblies should persist in their demands for control; the threat was at last fulfilled when Grenville embarked upon this new adventure with his revenue act designed to include the widest possible range of colonial interests. Whereas by his enforcement of commercial regulation Grenville had aroused the opposition of particular colonial merchants and had raised the question of parliamentary control of trade, now by the Stamp Act he opened several other fields of controversy. The broad scope of the act touched the pockets of merchants, lawyers, and journalists, and also involved a serious drain of currency. The principle of parliamentary taxation was itself a fertile source of speculation, leading to the related problem of the authority of parliament over the internal affairs of a colony. The spokesmen of America found it necessary to do some hard thinking on the nature of government and the status of colonies.

Practical grievances were at first met by practical measures of opposition, but it soon became advisable to seek justification in constitutional principles. So, on the basis of the rights of Englishmen, the Americans claimed that they should not be taxed by parliament, but only by the assemblies in which they were represented. Before these arguments had gone very far, the activity of English and American merchants made it possible for the Rockingham ministry to repeal the Stamp Act and replace it by the mere declaration of parliamentary supremacy. But when in 1767 Charles Townshend revived the demand for revenue in a form more subtle to resist, American political thinking advanced to the point of denying the authority of the existing English parliament over internal American affairs. As in seventeenth-century England, the abstract limitation of authority proved an unsatisfactory basis for practical redress. Some thinkers proceeded to suggest a reconstituted imperial legislature with colonial representation. Others preferred a recognized autonomy, which might include voluntary submission to the control by parliament of genuinely imperial concerns. By 1770 the tendency was to renounce parliament entirely, preserving only an allegiance to the king as sovereign over American and English subjects alike. One step alone remained, that of disowning the king and declaring independence. All except this could be maintained on high constitutional grounds; and the American arguments were thrown into the arena where George III was already struggling with Burke and Wilkes.[3]

The authority of parliament was the central issue of the American Revolution, and American claims were directed to justify resistance by limiting or denying that authority. The extent and nature of opposition varied with times and with persons, but not the goal of the attack. In England, however, parliamentary supremacy had become the accepted basis of political thinking, which whigs and tories of the new dispensation shared. George III and Rockingham met here on common ground. The supremacy of parliament had been a whig creation. Executive and legislative power had been merged in "the crown in parliament." The whig system of patronage had made ministers the agents of parliamentary authority, the universal validity of which the descendants of Walpole had no desire to impair since it formed the basis of their own aristocratic monopoly. George III had accepted the system, but had intervened to turn it to his own uses. No political leader was more insistent than he in upholding the full supremacy of parliament. The American challenge to this supremcy therefore found no response from either of the main combatants in the struggle for power, whigs or new tories. Only from the political heretics in England could the colonists win wholehearted support.

There still remained a few old tories who had not given their hearts to the sovereignty of crown-in-parliament, and who retained the idea of a king who could exercise the powers of the crown without

---

[3] R. G. Adams, *Political Ideas of the American Revolution* (Durham, N. C., 1922); C. H. McIlwain, *The American Revolution* (New York, 1923); R. L. Schuyler, *Parliament and the British Empire* (New York, 1929); C. F. Mullett, *Fundamental Law and the American Revolution* (New York, 1933); R. A. Humphreys, "The Rule of Law and the American Revolution," *Law Quarterly Review,* CCIX (1937):80–98.

inevitable recourse to parliamentary ministers. To these there might appear the prospect of such an imperial relationship as came later in the form of a commonwealth of nations united by the personal sovereignty of the king. Some of the clearest statements of this possibility occur in letters of Boswell, written after the war was in full swing: "I regret," he wrote to Johnson, "that the king does not see it to be better for him to receive constitutional supplies from his American subjects by the voice of their own assemblies . . . than through the medium of his British subjects. I am persuaded that the power of the crown, which I wish to increase, would be greater when in contact with all its dominions than if 'the rays of regal bounty' were to 'shine' upon America through that dense and troubled body, a modern British parliament."[4] "I have professed myself," he wrote to Burke, "a friend to our fellow-subjects in America, so far as they claim an exemption from being taxed by the representatives of the king's British subjects. . . . I deny the Declaratory Act; and I am a warm tory, in its true constitutional sense."[5] Boswell was right in calling this a tory solution. As Lord North told his critics in the House of Commons, the Americans talked of their belonging to the crown. "Their language therefore was that of toryism."[6]

It is an ironical fact that George III, instead of assuming the role of despot in which the whigs so persistently saw him, preferred the ignoble ascendancy of a parliamentary boss. He deliberately identified himself with parliamentary authority over America, and announced quite truly that he was "fighting the battle of the legislature."[7] Once again the king had stolen whig thunder. "The asserting an unlimited sovereignty over America," declared Courtenay in 1781, " . . . was a Whig principle, maintained by Whig statesmen, and confirmed by repeated acts of a Whig parliament."[8] The whig defense of America was made the more embarrassed and awkward by the danger of accidental agreement with old tories. No true whig could advocate an

---

[4] *Life of Samuel Johnson,* under date of Feb. 28, 1778.

[5] *Correspondence of the Rt. Hon. Edmund Burke,* Earl Fitzwilliam and Sir Richard Bourke, eds. (London, 1844), II:209.

[6] *Parliamentary History,* XVIII: 771.

[7] *Correspondence of King George III,* ed. Sir John Fortescue (London, 1928), III, No. 1709.

[8] *Parliamentary History,* XXI:1281.

enlargement of royal prestige and power; and meanwhile the king proceeded to uphold parliamentary sovereignty over the colonies by force.

While a few old tories might find themselves strangely associated with the colonists in their desire to see a monarchical power free from complete dependence on the will of parliament, there were others whose sympathies with America were less negative. An increasing number of radical thinkers rejected parliamentary supremacy, or at least the supremacy of the existing parliament, not to restore the king, but to elevate the people. Wilkes the politician, Price and Priestley the popular philosophers, and Cartwright the propagandist held different shades of disbelief in a supreme parliament, but all emphasized the sovereignty of the people and were not afraid to tamper with the constitution in order to restore its ancient purity. They tended therefore to regard the American claims as just and feasible. It is true that many radicals were not opposed in principle to the authority of a sovereign legislature, provided it were fully representative. Some might even go so far as to insist on the right to tax the colonies while at the same time demanding great changes in the structure of parliament.[9] But, like all rebels against the existing order, the reformers began by attacking the complete authority of the institution they wished to reform, and this involved a presumptive sympathy with its other enemies. It was to their interest to work together; and English radicals usually accepted the proffered hand, even if, as with Wilkes, their original enthusiasm for the American cause was not above suspicion.[10]

In appealing to the constitutional rights of Englishmen against a parliament that had failed in its trust the reformers allied themselves not only with American whigs, but also with Chatham. Chatham's position in the American controversies is of special significance, and seems to have been more consistent than the harsh criticism of some historians would suggest. It recalls the early stages of resistance to the Stuarts, when attempts were made to restrain the king within the bounds of law. Chatham retained this belief in a fundamental law,

[9] See, e.g., *An Historical Essay on the English Constitution* (London, 1771).
[10] Alexander Stephens, *Memoirs of John Horne Tooke* (London, 1813), I:178; *The Controversial Letters of John Wilkes* (London, 1771), pp. 161–167; D. M. Clark, *British Opinion and the American Revolution* (New Haven, 1930), chap. vi.

embodied in the English constitution, and expressed by Magna Carta
and the Bill of Rights. When the American whigs sought to restrain
parliament with the same constitutional argument, he rejoiced that
America had resisted.[11] He appealed to the constitution against the
House of Commons in the Middlesex election; he invoked it against
Lord Mansfield's judgment denying to juries the power of determin-
ing libels; and he upheld it against the Declaratory Act, which plainly
asserted the rival doctrine of parliamentary supremacy.[12] Moreover,
Chatham's proposals to admit the limitation of parliamentary authority over America might well have produced a solution of the colonial
problem, even though based on outmoded or untenable theories of
government. Backed by his own great reputation in the colonies,
Chatham was more likely to succeed than any other English statesman.
His vision, shared by Conway and Thomas Pownall, as well as by his
immediate followers, was of a great empire in which the English
parliament was willing to respect the limitation of its sovereignty.
It is difficult to see the feasibility at this time of any other kind of home
rule.

So far as the American problem could have been met on constitutional grounds, the greatest hope of conciliation would seem to have
rested in the limitation of parliamentary supremacy as advocated by
Chatham and the radicals. The Rockingham whigs, however, were
the staunch upholders of that supremacy, and although they could
unite with the others against the practical effects of royal patronage, the
common front did not extend to their interpretation of the imperial
relationship. On that subject the whigs agreed with the king. They
continued to insist on the authority of parliament, and their only hope
of opposing the ministerial policy lay in nullifying the effect of their
insistence on sovereignty by practical and voluntary conciliation. Their
attitude to American taxation was the same as that to the assertion of
parliamentary rights in England. When the House of Commons used
its privilege to attack the publication of its debates, Burke, unlike
Chatham, admitted the right but sought to temper its assertion. "You

---

[11] *Anecdotes of the Life of the Rt. Hon. William Pitt, Earl of Chatham* (London, 1793),
II:46.

[12] *Ibid.*, II:226–229, 343; Albemarle, *Memoirs of the Marquis of Rockingham* (London, 1852), II:261–262.

are not bound to exercise every right you possess," he declared. "Your prudence should regulate the exercise of your power."[13] This therefore became the whig program. They proclaimed their distaste for theoretical propositions and *a priori* reasoning, but they clung to the theoretical supremacy of parliament. At first the difficulties could be dissolved by the mere redress of actual grievances. But when the controversy was revived, this became less easy. There may have been little practical difference between denying the authority of parliament and retaining it unused. By emphasizing expediency rather than right Burke undoubtedly introduced a more profitable concept into the theory of government;[14] but at least the Rockingham whigs lagged behind Chatham in the apparent generosity of their proposals for peace. The Americans were always more lukewarm toward them than toward Chatham, to whom they persistently gave credit which the rival whigs regarded as their due. Personal friction magnified differences which might otherwise have been surmounted.

In 1765, when the first Rockingham ministry had been formed, the groupings of party were still uncertain and fluctuating, and whig policy toward America was determined to a large extent by the need of political support. The right of taxation was discussed and affirmed. Thus conservative members were conciliated. But when it became a question of repealing the Stamp Act or retaining it in modified form, repeal was the policy demanded by the two powerful elements which the government needed most to please, namely, Pitt and the merchants. Whatever therefore may have been their own preferences, Rockingham and his friends worked for repeal, and carried their point in February, 1766. Quiet was restored to America and the merchants by the removal of a practical grievance.

In order to avoid the impression that repeal was a surrender of parliamentary supremacy over the colonies, the Rockingham ministry had prefaced their action by declaratory legislation to affirm that supremacy "in all cases whatsoever." The famous Declaratory Act of 1766 was an interpretation which ran counter to the burning convic-

---

[13] *Sir Henry Cavendish's Debates* (London, 1841), II:388.
[14] F. T. H. Fletcher, *Montesquieu and English Politics* (London, 1939), pp. 205, 209–210. In this sphere, at least, Burke's principles flatly contradict Goldsmith's characterization of him as "too fond of the right to pursue the expedient."

tions of Chatham and of his friend Lord Camden, the great lawyer. One of the cardinal principles of their constitutional theory was the separation of government and taxation. Taxation, they declared, was no part of the governing or legislative power.[15] Americans, like Englishmen, could claim the inviolable right of property, which Locke had regarded as an essential liberty. From this time on, Chatham's hatred of the Declaratory Act never dwindled. The whigs sought to minimize its importance, and suggested that it was but the price of repeal, paid to the authoritarian majority. To Chatham the act was a perpetual violation of the rights of Englishmen, and he never forgave its authors.

The Declaratory Act disturbed Chatham more than the Americans. As yet, practical remedies could redress practical grievances without too close examination of their principles. The following year, however, saw the controversy reopened. The whigs were not blameless, for by a clever stroke of politics they had forced a reduction in the land tax, and the budget needed fresh sources of revenue. Charles Townshend introduced his famous American duties, and they evoked a more comprehensive theory of opposition from the colonies. The new duties were not burdensome in the degree that Grenville's impositions had been, nor were they strictly internal taxes. They therefore provoked a more sweeping attack on parliamentary authority instead of reviving the mere objection to taxation. In short, the Americans were approaching the English radical position where it was difficult for the whigs to support them.

Rockingham and his friends were by now out of office and without direct responsibility for American policy, but they had to consider what should be their stand as a group on the urgent matter of the Townshend duties. The ministry was apparently more hostile to the colonies than hitherto, and the resignations of Chatham and Shelburne completed the shift begun by the accession to office of the Bedford party. In the summer of 1768, Rockingham appealed to Dowdeswell for a plan of campaign, and Dowdeswell replied with a confidential statement of his ideas, hastily put to paper. Assuming that the agitation at Boston should become general, he said, the problem

---

[15] *Anecdotes of ... William Pitt*, II:35–36; *Parliamentary History*, XVI:177–181.

was that a principle seemed now to be involved on which it was difficult for England to yield. The Townshend duties could not be called
grievous, although they might be regarded as injudicious; but it would
be difficult to evade the issue of principle and the dilemma which it
presented. In this dilemma Dowdeswell blamed Chatham for his folly
in encouraging American resistance, Townshend for the imprudence
of reviving the controversial subject by a "foolish tax upon our own
manufactures," and the crowd of place seekers near the court for their
reckless threats against America. The situation was "distressful," and
the remedy did not lie in whig hands.

There was, in Dowdeswell's view, little hope that the matter would
be presented in a shape to encourage conciliation. The Americans were
"enthusiastic" and "liberty-mad." Their petitions would probably in-
volve claims amounting to a charter of freedom from all parliamentary legislation, and could not be supported by the whigs. "They
have no pretence to relief if they combine their grievance with their
principle, but I am afraid they will never separate them." If by a
remote chance the petitions should be moderate, and the colonists
should prudently confine their objections to the particular hardship
of a particular duty, then the whigs might safely return to their policy
after the Stamp Act and support the claim for repeal.

The ministry, Dowdeswell went on, was made up of a mixture of
weakness, obstinacy, and self-interest; and if the initiative came from
that quarter, the whigs should exercise moderating counsels, remem-
bering that the Bedford group had agreed on the need of moderation
as well as of authority. But they could not avoid the obvious duty of
the government to enforce the laws, and must be content to advocate
conciliation, provided the colonies first submitted. Between the two
disastrous choices of the surrender of all authority and the great losses
which war would bring, the whigs must use their influence for moderation. The duties should be repealed, if possible, but the principle of
exemption could not be admitted. If the worst should happen, and the
extremes of concession and enforcement become the only alternatives,
then let the whigs try to choose the lesser evil. But Dowdeswell was
conscious that his opinion could not be definite or final on this question, "the most difficult I ever knew"; and he urged Rockingham to

keep his counsel.[16] This advice was in complete accord with the inclinations of Rockingham himself, who admitted that he felt "just as angry at the dangerous madness of some in America as at the passion and obstinacy of some at home."[17] So when parliament met in November, 1768, the whigs confined themselves to questioning ministerial competence. Ministers had the responsibility, and they, said Dowdeswell, must answer for the results. The basis of parliamentary authority could not be challenged.[18]

The middle ground of whiggism in this early period of the American crisis is illustrated also in the attitude taken by another Rockingham whig, Richard Champion of Bristol. Writing to his relatives in America, he treated the problem almost entirely as one of trade. George Grenville had struck fatal blows at the commerce of the empire, and the Grafton ministry had repeated the error. The chief concern of the Rockingham whigs was to remove intolerable restrictions on trade. But America also laid herself open to criticism by failing to discriminate, in nonimportation agreements, between ministry and merchants. "She should have levelled her resentment upon administration, who really oppressed her, and not upon the commercial and manufacturing part of the kingdom, who were always her best friends." The most promising policy was that of mercantile pressure from both sides, combined with a studied moderation in avoiding unconstitutional claims and violent methods.

As for the alleged parallel between the American cause and that of electoral reform in England, this was to Champion a false analogy. "We may possibly want a more equal representation ourselves," he wrote, "but only for the purpose of preventing the very great corruption which the great number of boroughs occasion by the easy access the crown has to them. But in an English constitution alterations are difficult and dangerous, and it is better to suffer smaller evils than run the risk of greater." Even in 1689 there had been more risk of losing liberty than of gaining it. Now, therefore, every effort of unbiased judgment and disinterested resolution should be put forth to restrain the popular opposition in both countries from rising into a flame too

---

[16] Dowdeswell MSS (Aug. 14, 1768).   [18] *Cavendish's Debates,* I:43.
[17] Albemarle, *op. cit.,* II:80.

difficult to quench. Thus Champion, writing in 1770,[19] was urging upon America essentially the same policy that Burke was prescribing for England in his famous manifesto published at that time. Both upheld constitutional moderation at home, and approached the colonial problem by the same path.

During these years of domestic crisis, it is impossible to separate whig policy toward America from that toward Wilkes and the radicals at home. In both controversies the whigs agreed that violence could not be justified, but that grievances existed in the invasion of established rights of civil and political liberty. Dowdeswell in 1768 refused to give up opposition merely because Mr. Otis might agree with him, and he proceeded to denounce the transfer of cases of treason from America to England, saying that crimes were local and should be tried locally—an argument which would appeal with equal force to the whig zealot and the tory country gentleman.[20] Burke took a similar line in 1770. Only a few weeks before, he had attempted to excuse the violence of the City of London, whose remonstrance against the neglect of its petition concerning the Middlesex elections had spared neither king, ministers, nor parliament. The American disorders were another symptom of the same disease. "Whenever the people are aggrieved," he declared, "they will be violent"; but this did not mean that grievances should never be redressed, and he attacked the attempt "to introduce into the administration of our justice a martial police."[21] The tendency of these attacks was to criticize the actual conduct of administration rather than to enter upon the finer points of the colonial relationship. "The folly of the administration," said Burke, "has tended step by step to lead America into confusion."[22]

Almost at the time of publishing his *Thoughts on the Cause of the Present Discontents* Burke attempted a similar formulation of whig criticism in regard to American policy. On May 9, 1770, he moved for an inquiry into the causes of American disorders, and the theme of his address was the administrative incompetence of those responsible for colonial government. For three years, he said, the whig opposition had

---

[19] G. H. Guttridge, *The American Correspondence of a Bristol Merchant*, Univ. Calif. Publ. Hist., XXII (1934):18, 22.
[20] *Cavendish's Debates*, I:36–37, 195.
[21] *Ibid.*, p. 308.   [22] *Ibid.*, p. 200.

abstained from any vexatious proceedings or inquiries which might have obstructed the ministerial plan of operations. America could not be governed, or American affairs administered, in parliament. "The characteristic of parliament is to establish general laws, to give general powers and large grants of public money. It is the part of administration to use those powers with judgment, to employ the supplies with effect. . . . The trust is a great one; but it is a trust that is necessary." From this assumption he proceeded to indict the incompetence, the inconsistency, and the weakness of ministers, who had sent ill-judged and irreconcilable orders to colonial governors, had provided terrorizing legislation which was not carried into effect, and had pledged the faith of the crown for the future leniency of parliament. "His Majesty . . . is to receive all the thanks for removing public burdens; and parliament all the odium of laying them on. . . . All is shaken to the foundation by the entire absence of common sense."[23]

In thus founding their American policy upon administrative responsibility rather than raise the basic problem of authority, the whigs tacitly recognized the fact that they were in a difficult position. They would not join Chatham in restricting the supremacy of parliament on grounds of constitutional law. Still less would they advocate a reorganization of the representative system to satisfy popular or colonial desires. And yet they admitted the provocation of serious grievances at home and in America. Their only course was to attack the actual conduct of the existing ministry, and by so doing lay themselves open to the charge of factious opposition.

Ever since the formation of Chatham's miscellaneous administration in 1766, the political confusion was such as to encourage the cry of faction. Chatham's illness produced a state of chronic uncertainty and intrigue, in which the Rockingham whigs played their part by negotiations with Bedford and Grenville. "Continual cabals, factions, and intrigues among the outs and ins," wrote Franklin, "keep everything in confusion."[24] Thomas Pownall, revising his *Administration of the Colonies* for its fourth edition in 1768, introduced a new note of urgency into his earlier plea that American affairs should not fall

---

[23] *Cavendish's Debates,* II:14–24.
[24] A. H. Smyth, *The Writings of Benjamin Franklin* (New York, 1906), V:25.

a prey to partisan divisions in England. In default of a national plan, he wrote, the colonies "will for some time belong to some faction here, and be the tool of it, until they become powerful enough to hold a party for themselves, and make some faction their tool." After reading this, Burke scribbled in the margin of his own copy: "Has this paragraph any particular meaning? It seems to squint at some particular set of men."[25]

The attempted coalition between Rockingham, Bedford, and Grenville fell through, and the ministry was reconstituted on lines which included the more authoritarian imperialists in the government. For a while the American problem seemed to divide ministry from opposition, but the charge of faction was still freely bandied. And when once more Burke and Grenville found themselves in temporary alliance against Lord North, that imperturbable minister inquired pointedly whether, since their sole remedy for American disorders was a change of ministry, he should yield to those who had passed the Stamp Act or to those who had repealed it.[26]

Whig inactivity in American affairs between 1770 and 1774 appears at first sight to require some explanation, even though it was but part of a lull which pervaded the entire country. Whig fortunes were at a low ebb during this period.[27] The break with Chatham had been followed by divisions and defections; and the miscellaneous elements, united only in opposition to the ministry, added to the appearance of a purely factious desire for places. The association of the whigs with the rights of property at home, in Ireland, and in the East India Company gave little opportunity for rallying wide support.

There was, moreover, a convergence of opinion on American affairs. The king and the whigs both sought to maintain the authority of parliament. Chatham wished to preserve it as a governing power without violating the constitutional safeguards of property against taxation. There was little practical difference between Chatham's insistence that parliament had no right to tax America and Burke's desire to preserve the right but to refrain from exercising it. Even within the ministry

---

[25] Pownall, *Administration of the Colonies* (4th ed.), pp. 29–30. Burke's copy, with his MS notes, is in the British Museum.

[26] *Cavendish's Debates,* II:26, 31.

[27] See above, p. 46.

the hope of taxation was dwindling, and Franklin commented in 1771 that the doctrine was almost generally given up. All that remained was the dignity of parliament and the refusal to recede as far as a formal renunciation.[28]

The final blow to a whig program of resistance on American affairs came in 1772 with the appointment of Lord Dartmouth as secretary of state in charge of the colonial department. Dartmouth was a former member of the Rockingham ministry and had preserved a close connection with the group. His integrity was above suspicion, and his desire for conciliation well known. His acceptance of office was therefore a very different matter from the defection of Germain and Cornwall about the same time. It was rather the carrying of whig policies into the ministerial camp, the more since the intimacy of Dartmouth with North gave good reason for the belief that his conciliatory disposition was shared in higher quarters. With Dartmouth in the office principally concerned with America, instead of the harsh and authoritarian Hillsborough, the whigs could hardly launch a successful campaign against the ministry.

The basic unanimity of English opinion was shown when news of the Boston Tea Party arrived. The country was aroused, and the issue was reduced to one of authority. "The conduct of the Americans cannot be justified," said Rockingham, "but the folly and impolicy of the provocation deserves the fullest arraignment."[29] Only with the coming of penal measures could the whigs gain ground for attack. The ministerial policy of coercion began in March, 1774, with the Boston Port Act; and at first there was little effective opposition. "We all agree that the Bostonians should be punished," declared Rose Fuller, "but we differ in the mode of it."[30] At best it was urged that nothing hasty or irrevocable should be done; Boston should be heard and given the chance to make reparation. Rockingham, Burke, and Dowdeswell cautiously supported the American cause, but they were conscious of even less ardent feelings among their own supporters. They were greatly concerned, therefore, to avoid the appearance of perpetual and factious opposition when opinion was not ripe for success. They tried

---

[28] Smyth, *op. cit.*, V:292.
[29] *Correspondence of Edmund Burke*, I:449–450.
[30] *Parliamentary History*, XVII:1176–1177.

to shun all association with the "paltry discontented people" who recognized the advantages of their connection as the backing for personal ambitions.[31] They considered withdrawing from parliament until the issue was clear, adopting the position of spectators while the ministry set forth its American campaign, and retaining their influence for the future by refraining from conduct that would be labeled partisan.[32]

The later coercive acts brought more unity into opposition, as they seemed to carry the assertion of authority too far; and even the whig peers came out strongly against the ministry. But throughout the session of 1774 the conduct of the Rockingham whigs was tactical rather than constructive on the American question. They were likely to find one or more of their leaders with the ministry on any particular measure; and were glad to raise opposition on technical points of misrepresentation, in order to move with the full support of those friends "who might hesitate at the assertion of our American principles."[33] In May, on the third reading of the Bill for the Impartial Administration of Justice in Massachusetts Bay, Rockingham made one of his rare long speeches, "and never was more attention given to a speaker on any occasion." Declaring that the taxation of America had been a deviation from the ancient policy of Great Britain, he made clear his preference for repeal; but the main impression given by his speech was that of a calm appeal for moderation. "He concluded with a very emphatical recommendation of temper," says the *Parliamentary History;* "his own remarkable calmness and steadiness of mind gave additional force to this part of his speech."[34]

Later in the year, Rockingham explained to one of his followers the ideas which lay behind this insistence on moderation and on practical, rather than theoretical, policies toward America. "The point in controversy between this country, and the colonies," he wrote,[35] "will never be adjusted by explicit declarations on either side; and if ever a conciliation is brought about, it will be by much remaining unascertained, and by a conviction on one side, and by a confidence on the other, that similar disputes were neither politic nor practicable, and would never be revived again." Confessing that he had never been

---

[31] *Correspondence of Edmund Burke,* I:452.
[32] Albemarle, *op. cit.,* II:242.   [34] XVII: 1351.
[33] *Ibid.,* pp. 240–241.   [35] Albemarle, *op. cit.,* II:253–254.

able to draw a line limiting the extent of parliamentary authority over the colonies, he sought a solution on the basis of consent. "I don't love to claim a right on the foundation of the supreme power of the legislature over all the dominions of the Crown of Great Britain; I wish to find a consent, and acquiescence in the *governed,* and I choose therefore to have recourse to what I think an original *tacit compact,* and which usage has confirmed, until the late unhappy financiering project interrupted the union and harmony which had so long prevailed." Such an attitude reveals the characteristic whig virtue of conciliation, combined with an equally characteristic inability to realize the inadequacy of a mere return to the past.

Burke had already delivered the first of his great speeches on America; but it was not published until 1775, when, so the preface declared, the measures of government had had free opportunity to operate.[36] It is a tribute to the genius of Burke that here, as in his later speech on conciliation, the reader can never be quite sure whether the note of expediency, which he sounded throughout, was superlative statesmanship or superlative politics. He convicted the ministry of committing the very faults they deplored in the policy of conciliation, since they had repealed all the offending duties except that on tea. He justified the Rockingham ministry for its earlier policy of repeal, and also, be it noted, for the Declaratory Act. He proclaimed the interests of trade against those of revenue, to which the merchants were being sacrificed. And by his famous description of Chatham's mosaic ministry of 1766 he endangered the alliance which might have saved the empire. Once more the cause of parliament and the party came first, because that cause was to Burke the only sure basis of sound practical policy.

The ministerial measure which evoked the greatest harmony in whig opposition was the Quebec Act. The last important bill of the session, it had to bear the full brunt of a hostility which each successive measure of coercion against the colonies had deepened. Moreover, it aroused those Protestant passions which were still potent on the whig side. "The Quebec affair," wrote the Rev. Dr. Wilson from Bristol, "has given an amazing turn within these three weeks to the tame dispositions of the Quakers and Dissenters, who before that time

---

[36] *Parliamentary History,* XVII:1215 ff.

were fast asleep; but this has roused them. . . . "[37] For these reasons the violence of the whigs is not surprising.

When the Quebec Bill first came before parliament in May, 1774, it faced unqualified and unanimous opposition from whigs and radicals. Only the grounds of attack varied with different individuals. Some denounced the acceptance of the Roman Catholic faith as the religion of the colony; others attacked the appointive council, which replaced an elected assembly; others, the establishment of French civil law; and all, the extension of the area of the province to include the back country west of the English colonies. On the whole, the Rockingham whigs were the more moderate in their attacks. Burke carefully refrained from raising the religious issue, and he and his friends led a campaign directed chiefly against the constitutional provisions of the bill. The governmental provisions were in their view reactionary, and even indicated a "legal parliamentary despotism," fortified by the revenues of Quebec, at the uncontrolled disposal of the treasury. The mode of thought in these arguments is further shown by Burke's allusion to the people whom he regarded as affected by the bill. These were, in order, English merchants, English subjects, and Canadians. While, therefore, the Rockingham whigs may have represented the more conservative opposition, it is clear that they were thinking primarily of English commercial and constitutional interests.[38] By far the loudest argument was the cry of "despotism," the time-honored whig war cry; and Burke with all his moderation can hardly have appreciated the critical situation of British power in Canada when he proposed a year's delay in the consideration of the bill. The main grounds of opposition were constitutional, but the whigs were now thinking also of the American point of view. In this respect, therefore, the way was opening for America to be made the main rallying point of opposition.

There was little essential change in the new parliament. The court chose its own time for an election and succeeded in obtaining a new lease of power. The opposition groups had no cause for satisfaction, and the rest of 1774 was uneventful so far as any concerted attempts to

[37] *Correspondence of Edmund Burke,* I:466.
[38] *Parliamentary History,* XVII:1398.

change American policy were concerned. There was as yet no crisis sufficient to arouse public feeling, nor did the whigs expect any for some time. Thus from a combination of circumstances a full half year was wasted at the most critical stage of policy and opposition. The body of merchants showed no energy. Deterred by reluctance to oppose the ministers, and by dislike of organized faction, they abandoned the cause of opposition more completely, according to Burke, than he ever remembered. The great landowners tended to fall into inertia. "We can do no good," wrote the Duke of Richmond; "I grow very sick of politics."[39] Dowdeswell was taken ill. Sir George Savile talked of retiring; and in Burke's opinion, had he carried out his threat, the party would have been unable to maintain its existence.[40] Rockingham himself doubted whether he could properly encourage others to continue such hopeless political drudgery.[41]

Burke was almost alone in pressing for a plan of activity, against the inclination of other leaders who were again recommending a secession from parliament as their best policy. He urged Rockingham to take a firm stand. Disappointed as he was by the lack of public support, he realized that public opinion needs active leadership, and that in default of some initiative from the whigs the ministry would be supported for sheer lack of an alternative. "If your lordship should see things in this light," he wrote, "you will of course perceive too the necessity of proceeding regularly, and with your whole force; and that this great affair of America is to be taken up as a business."[42]

The idea of leaving the ministry unchecked was slow in dying, and Burke spent at least one sleepless night over the reluctance of whig leaders to resume active opposition. "The question . . . is," he told Rockingham, "whether your lordship chooses to lead or to be led."[43] However, when parliament reassembled in January, 1775, it was in a session which finally decided for the coercion of the colonies; and from this time on, for good or ill, the whigs concentrated their energies on America. Lord North submitted papers describing the disturbances

---

[39] *Correspondence of Edmund Burke,* I:485.
[40] *Ibid.,* p. 470.
[41] A. S. Turberville, *A History of Welbeck Abbey and Its Owners* (London, 1939), II: 139–140.
[42] *Correspondence of Edmund Burke,* I:505.
[43] *Ibid.,* p. 517.

of the past year, and proceeded to bring forward measures calculated to repress the offending Americans. Early in February the bill for restraining the trade of New England was introduced, and before it had passed the third reading a similar measure extended the prohibition to the southern colonies, in spite of the minister's argument that the first was an experiment.

These ministerial measures were from the beginning strenuously opposed. Lord Chatham, conscious of his unrivaled prestige, prepared to take the lead in opposition. Unfortunately, confident as ever that there could be no possible justification for any opinion different from his own, he was unwilling to work with Rockingham. At least ten days before parliament met, the two discussed the situation, and Rockingham was alarmed to find that Chatham seemed inclined to air their disagreement over the Declaratory Act. This was especially unfortunate since the American congress had not chosen to attack it, and to bring it up to cause dissension at home was a gratuitous stirring up of unnecessary discord. The whigs, however, decided not to compete in any way, but to leave Chatham with the initiative, supporting him wherever possible.[44] Chatham's attitude to them is revealed by his statement to Shelburne that, "having had no communication of purposes from others, I have made none to any." He seems, in fact, deliberately to have indulged his theatrical taste for surprise, asking Stanhope to spread the news that he was to make a motion, but keeping its purport to himself.[45]

On January 20, without consulting the whigs upon the details of his motion, Chatham moved for the withdrawal of the troops from Boston, as a preventive measure which would allow animosities to subside, or at least prevent a catastrophe. In the main his arguments were those with which the whigs could concur—the ordinary rights of the whig, in America as in England. Chatham did, however, as Rockingham feared, bring up the Declaratory Act as an obstacle to peace; and the whig leader was obliged to counter the charge and refer the subject to another occasion, while his friend Richmond sought a middle ground by considering the Declaratory Act expedient

[44] Albemarle, *op. cit.*, II:261–267.
[45] *Correspondence of William Pitt, Earl of Chatham* (London, 1839), IV:371, 375.

rather than right. Shelburne, supporting Chatham, saw fit to disclaim any political connections and to judge the subject on its merits.[46] The motion was lost by 68 to 18, the minority being smaller, according to Burke, than it would have been if opposition had been properly organized and Chatham more communicative. "The duke of Richmond told me," wrote Horace Walpole, "that for two hours he could scarce resolve to vote for the motion."[47]

Ten days later, Chatham followed up this hasty proposal by a more detailed proposition for peace; and in the manner in which it was prepared, and received, it followed closely its predecessor. The Duke of Richmond had tried to make himself a link between the two leaders of opposition and had suggested consultation about the debate which they must force. Richmond's desire for union was fruitless, however, and all that he received was the bare notice on January 31 that Chatham would make a proposal on the following day. Chatham repeated his previous instructions to Stanhope—to spread the report of an intended motion but not to divulge its nature. Again, therefore, the whigs had to dispense with all preparation.[48]

Chatham's proposal of February 1 proved to be an assertion of the supremacy of parliament over matters concerning the whole empire and beyond the competence of a local assembly, but a supremacy that did not include the right of taxation or the right to use a standing army for coercion—in other words, a supremacy restrained by fundamental law, and therefore not wholly congenial to the whigs. Congress was recognized, and authorized to make and appropriate a grant of perpetual revenue to the king. The penal acts were to be suspended as soon as the acknowledgment of authority was made. Once more, as if to advertise his disagreement with Rockingham, Chatham deprecated the idea of party and asked for the assistance of all to impose his measure. The opposition on this occasion mustered greater strength. On the ministerial side Dartmouth was sympathetic; and after Richmond and Manchester had expressed their general, though qualified, assent, the measure found 32 supporters against the ministerial vote of 61.[49]

---

[46] *Parliamentary History*, XVIII:149 ff.
[47] *Last Journals* (1859), I:447.
[48] Albemarle, *op. cit.*, II:265–267; *Correspondence of William Pitt*, IV:388–391.
[49] *Parliamentary History*, XVIII:198–215.

Apart from these proposals by Chatham, the opposition concerned itself mainly with denouncing the ministry and denying that the Americans were in rebellion. The Rockingham whigs found it necessary once more to disclaim notions of factious opposition and the cult of popularity. They showed no eagerness to associate themselves with American constitutional claims, and the merits of those claims were left to the followers of Chatham. In both houses the trend of votes was toward ministerial majorities of about 3 to 1; and the similarity of tactics in the two houses is confirmed by the fact that Burke, at Richmond's request, composed the protests of the dissentient peers. After the first few weeks, the ministry rallied even greater majorities, and from the middle of February the opposition could not muster more than approximately one vote in five. Notable among their deserters were Sir William Meredith, who had been prominent in the whig fight for liberty in the '60s, and Governor Pownall, who now assented to the punishment of the colonies in the interests of trade. Among those who remained the demand for a secession still continued.

The merchants also had again failed to provide the whigs with as much support as they expected. A large number of petitions accompanied Chatham's plans of conciliation ("What unaccountable manoeuvre checked the vigour of their first operation?" he asked, with a side thrust at the whigs);[50] but differences soon appeared on the propriety of petitioning at that time, and by August Burke was sadly admitting: "... we look to the merchants in vain—they are gone from us, and from themselves. They consider America as lost, and they look to administration for an indemnity."[51]

On February 20, Lord North introduced his plan of conciliation, which provided that if and when any colony made free and satisfactory grants to the imperial treasury it should not be taxed by parliament. The king's friends were startled by the plan, and some spoke against it. But if Lord North had failed to warn his own supporters of his conciliatory intentions, he had also neglected to forestall criticism by taking the opposition into his confidence, although he notified Burke that important American business was to come up.[52] The con-

[50] *Correspondence of William Pitt*, IV:386.   [52] *Ibid.*, II:23–24.
[51] *Correspondence of Edmund Burke*, II:49.

ciliatory proposals may have been entirely sincere, but, if so, their ultimate success was doomed by the impolitic mode of presentation, which insured the utmost suspicion. Whigs of both sections attacked the scheme as insidious, calculated to divide the colonies, and designed to extort revenue by requisitions which were in fact compulsory. They would have none of such conciliation. "Are these your friends?" asked the ministerial *Address to the Inhabitants of America.* "They threw behind them all your interests. They attended to those of their own Party alone, which they think are more concerned in defeating a Minister than saving a Nation."[53]

Lord North's proposal did not affect the bills to restrain colonial trade, which were pushed through their various stages. At the beginning of March, news from America, which reached the whigs through their mercantile connections, indicated the likelihood of submission;[54] and the opposition, fearing that this weakness would ruin their own cause, were subjected afresh to ridicule and charges of faction. Public opinion seemed to be turning against them; and Chatham, who in February had considered the country as a whole to be against the war, admitted a month later that even in the country outside parliament there might be a majority against America. The king certainly accounted thus for the languor of opposition.[55]

On the 22d of March, Burke, who for some weeks had been preparing a scheme of conciliation, introduced his resolutions. Faithful to the party's middle ground, he assumed the basis of parliamentary supremacy but denounced the taxing of America in the antechamber of the ministry, proposed the repeal of all offending legislation since 1767, and suggested that the only satisfactory contribution had come in the form of free grants. "The proposition is peace," he declared, "not peace to depend on the juridical determination of perplexing questions; or the precise marking the shadowy boundaries of a complex government. It is simple peace."[56]

The absence of any real hope of revenue in Burke's proposals was

[53] P. 59. For an interesting comment on the proposals and their reception, see also W. Pulteney, *Thoughts on the Present State of Affairs with America* (London, 1778), pp. 55–61.

[54] Guttridge, *The American Correspondence of a Bristol Merchant,* p. 45.

[55] *Correspondence of King George III,* III, No. 1612.

[56] *Parliamentary History,* XVIII:482.

regarded by the whigs variously as a merit and as a disadvantage. Catching at a vain hope of satisfying the revenue seekers, David Hartley attempted to supplement Burke's proposals by adding a plan of royal requisition.[57] At this proposal, Lord North could not resist the obvious opening to turn whig arguments against the party. Royal requisitions, he said, had the same objections that had been commonly asserted against ship money; and Sir George Savile had to come to the rescue of his protégé by arguing that the objection to ship money was not the demand, but the method of enforcing it. Such an incident illustrates the predicament in which the whigs frequently found themselves, their principles precluding any constitutional settlement of the colonial problem except on a parliamentary basis, while at the same time they advocated the practical nullification of parliamentary authority. Burke's plea that the "proposition is peace . . . simple peace" was a noble one, but it was also extremely convenient, for the whigs had nothing to offer except an appeal to Time the healer, the future being left to take care of itself. "After all," wrote Dean Tucker, "what is this heaven-born pacific scheme . . . ? Why truly: if we will grant the colonies all that they shall require, and stipulate for nothing in return; then they will be at peace with us. I believe it; and on these simple principles of simple peacemaking I will engage to terminate every difference throughout the world."[58]

This contemptuous treatment of whig policy came in the midst of a series of pamphlets in which Tucker advocated his own solution—that of separation—for the colonial relationship.[59] With some truth and much skill the dean showed up the weak places in whig armor. More than once he devoted some pains to refute the favorite whig assumption that relations between England and her colonies had been satisfactory before 1763. This "very strange notion," he declared, was directly contradicted by frequent colonial attempts to resist and evade the laws of trade, by the colonists' legislation in defiance of English authority, and by their evasion of debts owing to English merchants.

[57] *Ibid.*, pp. 552 ff.

[58] Josiah Tucker, *A Letter to Edmund Burke* (Gloucester, 1775), reprinted in R. L. Schuyler, ed., *Josiah Tucker: A Selection from His . . . Writings* (New York, 1931), p. 394.

[59] *Four Tracts* . . . (Gloucester, 1774), *Tract V* . . . (Gloucester, 1775), *An Humble Address and Earnest Appeal* . . . (Gloucester, 1775)—all reprinted in Schuyler, *op. cit.*

It was therefore a palpable absurdity to build the hopes of peace on a basis which history and experience showed to be false. Moreover, the whig opposition, said Tucker, should bear a considerable share of responsibility for the resistance which the Stamp Act provoked. By their letters to friends in America and by their organization of protests the whigs had actually stirred up the troubles which they later wished to allay. The Americans, however, had quickly learned the successful game and would continue to play it.[60]

Burke could meet this onslaught but weakly, by protesting that there was little parliamentary resistance to the Stamp Act. Since Tucker had not concerned himself with parliamentary proceedings, the defense was inadequate, as Burke may have realized when he distracted attention by an unjust attack on Tucker's personal ambitions.[61] Spurred on by this taunt, the dean took up Burke's proposals for peace and submitted them to a scathing analysis in which he claimed that the plan would transform each provincial assembly into an independent American parliament contributing as it pleased to the royal exchequer. In such a constitution there could be no other final arbiter than the crown, invested with power independent of parliament, and with a standing army adequate to enforce that power. Thus the whig proposals came round to defeat at the hands of their dearest enemy, the arbitrary power of the crown.

Tucker completed his denunciation of whig policy by the usual accusations of partisan self-interest. He drew attention to the alliance with the radicals, whom, he said, the whigs were using for their own advantage without any intention of assisting them to reduce aristocratic power. "You have a very difficult part to act," he told Burke. "Certain it is that both the American and the English Republicans expect great things from you: They expect that you would assist them in reducing the power of the Crown, and of the House of Peers to a mere Cypher;—or rather to abolish them totally, Root and Branch: And they expect likewise that you would co-operate with them in subjecting the House of Commons itself to the Instructions of Town-Meetings, select Meetings, Liberty-Meetings, etc. etc. etc. . . . On the

[60] *Four Tracts* . . . (Gloucester, 1774), pp. 180–181.
[61] *Parliamentary History*, XVII:1253.

other Hand, it is equally certain, that you are endeavouring to make use of these factious Republicans, as the Tools and Instruments of your own Advancement, without gratifying them in their darling Object." These were the opinions of a dissentient whig, biased and exaggerated no doubt, but entitled to a hearing beside the rhetoric of Burke, which, to Tucker, "ended in noise and smoke."[62]

During the summer of 1775 the weakness of whig organization became only too apparent. Burke with his usual sagacity saw that the great aim should be to prevent the complete entanglement of parliament in the ministerial policy of coercion. By striving to keep responsibility centered in the administration, and by thwarting the union of king and parliament in the new tory system, the whigs might hope to preserve for parliament that independence which still appealed to the country gentlemen, and which would also provide a basis for the defeat of the ministry as soon as opportunity offered. No time ought to be lost, he urged Rockingham, for if parliament were to meet early and commit itself to war the damage would be beyond redress. The whigs must strain every effort to prevent this "full and decided engagement of parliament in this war." Rockingham and the Cavendishes, however, did not see what could be done. They therefore proposed to wait until parliament had rejected their plea for conciliation, and then make some kind of protest.[63]

Burke turned to the more active sympathies of Richmond and Portland, but the best course was not plain. Portland suggested that the whig difficulty lay in the suspicion of their being too radical, and that their program ought to include the clear assertion of the superintending authority of England over America.[64] Sir George Savile was more concerned lest the whigs by their activity should drive the ministry on and break down a bridge which the waverers might still cross.[65]

In November, Burke brought forward his second plan of conciliation.[66] In it he recommended that most of the offending acts be repealed

---

[62] *An Humble Address and Earnest Appeal* . . . (Gloucester, 1775), pp. 5–6, 33–35; *A Letter to Edmund Burke* (Gloucester, 1775), reprinted in Schuyler, *op. cit.*, pp. 379–380.

[63] *Correspondence of Edmund Burke*, II:35, 41, 50, 66.

[64] *Ibid.*, pp. 71, 76.

[65] Albemarle, *op. cit.*, II:282–287.

[66] *Parliamentary History*, XVIII:963 ff.

and that a declaration be made by parliament renouncing the power of taxation over America as the king had renounced it in England without repudiating his own sovereignty. Once again Burke demonstrated his belief in the unrestricted authority of parliament, but he was now willing by formal action to renounce its exercise. "I have been a strenuous advocate for the superiority of this country," he had written to Champion earlier in the year, "but I confess I grow less zealous, when I see the use which is made of it."[67] The Declaratory Act was to remain; but a cautious step was taken toward the recognition of an American congress for specified purposes. A tolerable showing was made by the opposition: 105 votes were cast for Burke's scheme, 210 against it. This was the maximum of achievement for several years. Even so, if Horace Walpole is to be trusted, some friends of Chatham and Shelburne were offended and did not attend, since Burke made no mention of the Quebec Act, which they would have included among the undesirable acts to be repealed.[68]

Prior to November, 1775, the division and uncertainty among the whigs had been paralleled by division and uncertainty in the ministry. "Administration," wrote Thomas Hutchinson in February, "is tender, doubting and undetermined."[69] Cornwall, a new recruit to the ministry, described North as consulting so many different opinions that he himself remained undecided.[70] Lord Dartmouth was a friend to conciliation, and as long as he remained in the office which was chiefly concerned with colonial affairs the whigs were tempted to hope that an extreme course would be avoided. In November, 1775, however, Dartmouth was superseded in the secretaryship of state by Lord George Germain, a whig renegade who was recognized as the exponent of downright coercion. Indications soon appeared that the government was now insisting on unconditional submission, and the Duke of Grafton proposed to put this intention to the test. Grafton had signalized his appearance in opposition by a vigorous attack on the military policy of the government, and in March, 1776, he sought sanction for an announcement to the Americans that, if they would

---

[67] *Correspondence*, II:26.
[68] *Last Journals* (1859), I:521.
[69] *Diary and Letters of . . . Thomas Hutchinson* (London, 1883), I:375.
[70] *Ibid.*, I:404.

come forward with a petition as proposed in the earlier ministerial scheme, hostilities would be suspended at once, and their requests would receive careful consideration by the king.[71] Grafton's motion was designed as a last chance for the ministry to show a genuine desire for conciliation, and its rejection was hailed by contemporaries as of significance comparable only to the American declaration of independence which followed four months later. "No alternative now seemed to be left between absolute conquest and unconditional submission."[72]

The years 1776 and 1777 were dark ones for the whig opposition in parliament. Its unhappy plight had been described in the previous October by Sir George Savile. "The situation of men who prophesy bad," he wrote to Rockingham, "is always odious, for no man will believe they don't wish their words may prove true. I have no time here to enter into the question how far wishing them *bad success* is an odious wish, but on the face of it, it is wishing *calamity,* and at best, it is ... too transatlantic an idea to ground one's actions upon."[73] Conciliation with America had failed, war had aroused the clear-cut emotions of patriotism, and military reverses had not yet occurred to damp the national enthusiasm. The failure of Grafton's motion confirmed the insistence on unconditional submission which it had been designed to test, and all hope of influencing the ministry was gone. In fact, there was a positive danger that whig criticism might actually increase the animosity against America and the military preparations for coercion. Savile had this possibility in mind when he strongly urged upon Rockingham the policy of "melancholy silence."

"Too inconsiderable in numbers, weight and measures to hinder the progress of administration," the opposition was hard put to decide upon any concerted plan of action, and it was obvious that only with the most complete unity was there any hope of achievement. Several attempts had already been made to restore harmony between the two main groups. Immediately after parliament met in November, 1775, Dr. Joseph Priestley, librarian to Lord Shelburne, wrote to Sir George

---

[71] *Parliamentary History,* XVIII:1247 ff.; *Autobiography ... of Augustus Henry, Third Duke of Grafton* (London, 1898), p. 282.
[72] *Annual Register,* 1776, pp. 139–140.
[73] Albemarle, *op. cit.,* II:282–287.

Savile to say that Shelburne frequently expressed the desire to be in a closer understanding with him, and, if necessary, was prepared to act under Rockingham's leadership. He pointed out that Shelburne's American policy was more conciliatory than Rockingham's since it disowned the Declaratory Act, and he insisted that strenuous efforts must be made to get at the source of administrative influence. Savile replied that he had almost given up hope of united action and was glad to find an opening.[74]

About the same time, Rockingham on his part expressed a willingness to overlook differences and to forgive tricks. He wrote Camden to the effect that a mode of conduct might be arranged without any sacrifice of principles. Camden returned the desire for harmony and promised his support.[75] At the same time, Camden was reëstablishing close relations with the Duke of Grafton, who had already announced his disagreement with the ministry, and conversations with Shelburne followed.[76] A chain of amity was thus formed, with the weakest links at Rockingham's end, through Camden and Priestley. By January, 1776, when the various leaders were coöperating well, Admiral Keppel took a hand in the game of good will. He spent several days as Shelburne's guest at Bowood and reported the result to Rockingham, his friend and leader. It was clear that no substantial agreement lay behind the superficial harmony. Shelburne spoke freely to Keppel and regretted that Rockingham had not produced a policy that could be generally supported. The Rockingham whigs, he said "did not speak out." Keppel on his part suggested that Lord Chatham and his methods made coöperation very difficult; but Shelburne seemed to feel that Chatham was above criticism and must be paramount.[77]

The fatal division persisted, and was increased by the publication in February of one of the most famous English pamphlets of the decade. Richard Price's *Observations on the Nature of Civil Liberty,* although professedly the work of an unconnected philosopher, was written by a close friend and protégé of Shelburne, whose American policy and program of conciliation it commended. While attacking

---

[74] Historical MSS Commission, 15th Rept., App. V (Savile-Foljambe MSS), pp. 149–150.
[75] *Correspondence of Edmund Burke,* II:85; Albemarle, *op. cit.,* II:287–288.
[76] *Autobiography of . . . Grafton,* pp. 275–278.
[77] *Life of Augustus, Viscount Keppel* (London, 1842), I:420–423.

the ministry and defending the Americans, it laid down principles of government to which Burke and his friends could not assent. The omnipotence of parliament, said Price, was an absurd idea. "They possess no power beyond the limits of the trust for the execution of which they were formed. If they contradict this trust, they betray their constituents and dissolve themselves."[78] Authority resides in the people, and the same rights which are retained by the people against a privileged class or parliament are possessed by a political community against external authority. "A country that is subject to the legislature of another country, in which it has no voice, and over which it has no control, cannot be said to be governed by its own will. Such a country, therefore, is in a state of slavery."[79] Thus the radical attack on the supremacy of parliament was linked with American claims of self-government; and Price, in supporting Shelburne, advocated the relinquishment of English authority over colonial affairs, except for the regulation of imperial trade. As for the Declaratory Act, the formal assertion by the whigs of parliamentary supremacy, "I defy anyone," said Price, "to express slavery in stronger language."[80]

This "combustible piece," as Burke called it,[81] was highly inconvenient to the whigs. In the interests of a united front they might "let Dr Price rail at the Declaratory Act";[82] but they could not allow such heterodoxy to pass unchallenged, and within a year Burke himself took up the cudgels on behalf of parliamentary supremacy and aristocratic privilege. Among the conventionally patriotic and authoritarian, however, the whig opposition was inevitably tainted by the radicalism which Price's views associated with the American cause, and which was alleged to aim at "the total extirpation of monarchy and episcopacy."[83]

There was special reason for the increased fear of radicalism in 1776, for in that year there appeared in England a clear formulation of beliefs and claims comparable to those of America. Just as the Americans had passed from the position in which they demanded the constitutional rights of Englishmen to that of maintaining the far more revo-

---

[78] Price's *Observations* (2d ed.), p. 15.
[79] *Ibid.*, p. 19. [82] *Ibid.*, p. 98.
[80] *Ibid.*, p. 34. [83] *The Revolution Vindicated* (Cambridge, 1777).
[81] *Correspondence*, II:139.

lutionary "rights of man," so now English radicals were advancing to the same position. Whereas in 1769 they had advocated a restoration of the rights of electors and the summoning of frequent parliaments in accordance with the ancient custom of the land, now a few writers began to proclaim the more drastic right of individuals to a share in government. Whereas former advocates of reform had contented themselves at most with the abolition of some rotten boroughs and an increase in the membership for existing county constituencies, involving no necessary or considerable increase in the franchise, the demand now emerged for universal suffrage and a reconstruction of parliament.

Almost at the time when Price's pamphlet appeared, John Wilkes introduced in parliament a systematic plan of reform, and before the end of the year John Cartwright published *Take Your Choice,* the first manifesto in the cause to which he dedicated his life. Cartwright was a man of simple integrity, who rested his argument on "the most well-known principles of the English constitution ... the plain maxims of the law of nature and the clearest doctrines of Christianity."[84] Although he thus continued to appeal to the English constitution, it is clear that Cartwright was in fact extending his claims to attack the rights of property and proclaim those of persons. "The first and most natural idea," he wrote, "that will occur to any unprejudiced man, is, that every individual of them, whether possessed of ... property, or not, ought to have a vote in sending to parliament those men who are to act as his representatives."[85] The same simplicity which made him content with the "divine right of liberty" led him also to condemn any more compromising doctrine in public life. Prescriptive rights, so dear to Burke, were to him no better than the claims of Cornish wreckers, and any man in opposition who would not pledge himself to the cause of reform was nothing but a factious demagogue.[86] Cartwright, like Price, was a fervent champion of the American cause, and the whigs, caught between the patriotic and the radical fires, realized that their middle ground was less tenable than ever.

---

[84] *Life and Correspondence of Major Cartwright,* ed. F. D. Cartwright (London, 1826), I:65.
[85] *Take Your Choice,* p. 19.
[86] *Ibid.,* pp. 42–43, 61.

Meanwhile, events in America combined to frustrate their hopes. The publication of Paine's *Common Sense* in January, 1776, was soon followed by the Declaration of Independence. The time for mediation was over. "If the constitutional line is ever meant to be determinately drawn between this country and her colonies," wrote a pamphleteer in February, "it must be drawn now or never, for if America is to be brought up on all occasions as a political engine to shake and distress the councils of this nation, farewell to the boasted supremacy of this country."[87]

In these circumstances whig proposals were treated with more and more asperity. The Declaration of Independence made it necessary for them to explain away the American design of separation which they had consistently disowned. "What then are we?" wrote Camden to Grafton, "mere friends or enemies to America; friends to their rights and privileges as fellow subjects, but not friends to their independence."[88] The ministers, he went on, have turned a tyrannical invasion into a national and necessary war, and the opposition will now be called to unanimity as Englishmen. Camden's prophecy was amply fulfilled, and Lord Pelham voiced a typical opinion when he expressed the hope that opposition could not in conscience support the rebellious act of people who aimed at more power than their mother country.[89] In fact, the whigs accumulated much odium by insisting that the war was a civil war, in which those in England were free to choose their sides. Prominent officers refused to serve against the colonies, and those who had American friends continued to correspond with them, so far as they were able, even giving them information about military preparations in England.[90]

In the face of their increasing unpopularity, ineffectiveness, and disunion the whig leaders again considered the possibility of a secession from parliament. Rockingham, Portland, and Richmond all suffered from poor health, and were obliged at intervals to neglect their parliamentary duties. During his conversations with Keppel in Janu-

[87] *An Address to the People of Great Britain in General* ... (Bristol, 1776), p. 76.
[88] *Autobiography of ... Grafton*, p. 288.
[89] Add. MSS (Brit. Mus.), 33, 127.
[90] Sir G. O. Trevelyan, *The American Revolution* (New York, 1928), III:202–215; Guttridge, *American Correspondence of a Bristol Merchant*, pp. 5, 65.

ary, Shelburne had remarked that the inability of Lord Rockingham to produce a policy that all could support had induced many members of parliament to discontinue regular attendance.[91] Camden was discussing the subject with Grafton at the same time, and gave his opinion strongly for secession. If union could not be achieved, he said, the opposition had better not attend; they might thus give more appearance of harmony.[92]

As the session drew to its end, and the whigs had nothing to do but, as Grafton put it, "retire to their country seats and there meditate,"[93] the question of policy exercised many minds. In August, the Duke of Richmond went to France to put in order his French peerage of D'Aubigny; and he told Burke frankly that he was preparing a retreat for himself against the day when despotism should have made England intolerable and when America would not be open to the exile. "About English politics," he wrote, "I most freely confess to you that I am quite sick and wore out with the too melancholy state of them."[94] America had declared her independence. France might at any time declare war. What was then to be the fate of opposition?

Rockingham himself was evidently leaning toward the policy of withdrawing from parliament in protest and in appeal to the public; but it is characteristic of the utter confusion among the whigs that, when secession actually came, it failed to win the support even of some who had advocated it. The policy was strenuously opposed by Charles Fox on the ground that it would be running away from the American cause at a time when the Americans were meeting with reverses.[95] The whig aristocracy, however, had more weight than the young commoner, and after a final muster for an amendment to the address, and a defeat by the usual majority, the whigs withdrew for a demonstration of abstinence.

The secession of the whigs from parliament in November, 1776, was clearly a move desired by the more conservative and aristocratic, although Burke may have been largely responsible. For several years

[91] Keppel, *Life* . . ., I:421.
[92] *Autobiography of . . . Grafton*, p. 279.
[93] *Ibid.*, p. 287.
[94] *Correspondence of Edmund Burke*, II:112, 120.
[95] Albemarle, *op. cit.*, II:297.

the Rockingham group had seriously considered a policy of systematic nonattendance, at least during definitely ministerial debates, with the object of calling public attention to the overriding policy of the ministerial bloc. There had been considerable opposition, however, even to a temporary and restricted nonattendance, and Burke had regarded a formal secession from parliament as impracticable. The justification of such a policy was always controversial, both in principle and as a matter of strategy, but throughout the century secession remained a recognized, though drastic, method of disavowing ministerial policy.[96]

The whig secession which now took place was referred to by the Duke of Manchester as the last attempt of his party, and he expressed his determination to lament the decline of Britain in silence, since all active attempts were in vain.[97] As Rockingham's biographer put it, the whigs, considering that there was no saving a people against their will, "determined to reserve their exertions for a season when the national delirium should so far abate as to afford some hope of advantage."[98] Thus far the whig abstention came dangerously near the lethargy of despair; and in the actual mode of secession the whigs bungled characteristically. Horace Walpole avers that he suggested a secession the previous year, with the idea of a dramatic public protest; and now the step was taken, but inconspicuously, and without any appeal to the public.[99]

Possibly the absence of any strong declaration was due not only to temperamental reluctance, but also to the difficulty of obtaining the consent of all to such a protest. Actually, the followers of Chatham did not join in the withdrawal because, according to Arthur Lee, the Rockingham whigs would not agree to denounce the basic abuse of the constitution, but merely made the temporary misconduct of the ministry the reason for their action.[100] Camden and Grafton did not join the movement, although the former hesitated at first, as well he might, having been one of the principal advocates of secession. Fox coöperated to the extent of leaving for Paris; but he definitely dis-

---

[96] *Correspondence of Edmund Burke*, I:346, 356; *Wyvill Papers*, VI (App.).
[97] *Parliamentary History*, XVIII:1366 ff.
[98] Albemarle, *op. cit.*, II:304.
[99] *Last Journals* (1859), II:92.
[100] *Revolutionary Diplomatic Correspondence of the United States*, ed. Francis Wharton (Washington, 1889), II:193.

approved, as was natural in one who knew his strength as a parliamentarian.[101] Thus the short session before Christmas produced a policy more like an inglorious retreat than a public call to arms.

Early in January, 1777, the matter had to be considered seriously. The prospect of success for the ministerial policy in America brought Rockingham and Burke to the lowest pitch of despair. They saw the vast majority of the country's influence ranged against them, and considered the likelihood of being subjected to impeachment. Rockingham expressed great reluctance to leave his country home, and Burke agreed that the policy of secession ought to continue. There was no hope for the whigs in parliament; their only chance lay with the public outside.[102] Sir George Savile could not see even this hope, and to him the whigs were cheapening themselves by reiterating their views in parliament. "We are not only patriots out of place," he wrote, "but patriots out of the opinion of the public.... The cause itself wears away by degrees from a question of right and wrong between subjects, to a war between us and a foreign nation, in which justice is never heard, because love of one's country, which is a more favourite virtue, is on the other side." "We have been used," he went on, "to this consolation at the bottom of our cup, that we had the public opinion. It is hard to give it up. We have it not most certainly."[103]

Meanwhile the government took the king's advice to bring forward as much business as possible "when the attention of the house is not taken up by noisy declamations";[104] and by the middle of February the whig abstinence was put to a severe test. A bill was brought in to suspend the Habeas Corpus Act in cases of high treason, and the attack upon this pillar of whig liberties tempted all but the most determined seceders. The followers of Chatham were present in force, and Dunning carried an amendment of some value. Fox spoke early in the career of the bill. Conway was there, and even Sir George Savile could not resist the temptation to return. Rockingham, Burke, and the Cavendishes remained the only firm champions of the whig

---

[101] *Autobiography of ... Grafton*, pp. 279, 289–290; Lord John Russell, *Memorials and Correspondence of Charles James Fox* (London, 1853), I:144–149, 154.

[102] *Correspondence of Edmund Burke*, II:132; Burke, *A Letter to the Marquis of Rockingham* (Jan. 6, 1777).

[103] Albemarle, *op. cit.*, II:304.

[104] *Correspondence of King George III*, III, No. 1929.

scheme. Burke gave other reasons for staying away. He could not support the bill, he said, and he did not like the amendments. He still insisted, however, that attendance in parliament was serving the interest of the ministry more than that of opposition.[105] It is of little importance whether those whigs who still "adhered to their stupid retreat"[106] did so from belief in secession or disagreement with the other groups in opposition. The Duke of Richmond summed up the situation when he wrote to Rockingham on February 19 that the worst had happened, and the plan adopted had not been steadily pursued. Thus the whigs returned discredited to the unfavorable state they were in a year before; and Richmond could only reiterate the earlier advice of Savile and advocate, once more, "attendance and opposition upon great questions in a melancholy and desponding way."[107]

Burke's abstention from parliament during the proposed bill to suspend the Habeas Corpus Act was far from pleasing to his constituents at Bristol. He had never been the most popular of candidates; he lacked both the private fortune and the ministerial interest which might have enabled him to "nurse his constituency"; and already he had shown an independence which was disturbing to his friends.[108] Richard Champion had urged him to pay the city at least an occasional visit; and Burke had replied with that well-known criticism of the provincial standards of those constitutents who judged a member "solely by his merits as their special agent." Champion now represented to his friend the further cause of disaffection. Burke justified his conduct; but the bad impression persisted, and Champion urged him to do more.[109] The result was the famous *Letter to the Sheriffs of Bristol,* Burke's second manifesto designed to justify the policy of his party. Opposition in parliament, he declared, "rather inflamed than lessened the distemper of the public councils," and was "considered as factious by most within doors and by very many without." He then

[105] *Correspondence of Edmund Burke,* II:148; *Letter to the Sheriffs of Bristol* (London, 1777).
[106] Horace Walpole, *Last Journals* (1859), II:96.
[107] Albemarle, *op. cit.,* II:308.
[108] Ernest Barker, *Burke and Bristol* (Bristol, n.d.); G. E. Weare, *Edmund Burke's Connection with Bristol* (Bristol, 1894).
[109] *Correspondence of Edmund Burke,* II:148–151, 165–169; Hugh Owen, *Two Centuries of Ceramic Art in Bristol* (London, 1873), pp. 212–216.

proceeded to recount the folly of the war with America, in the course of which he repeated his assertion of the original supremacy of parliament in America as in England. He was unable, he said, to see how part of that supreme legislative power could be given up by abstract reasoning, without the rest being given up too. This dual defense precipitated another controversy, waged in print through the summer and autumn, and aroused once more those radical opinions which had been expressed a year before by Richard Price.

This time Burke's critic was the enthusiastic Earl of Abingdon, who was a devoted champion of the American cause both in theory and in practice. Abingdon's *Thoughts* on Burke's letter took him to task on the policy of nonattendance and sought to show that criticism in parliament had actually produced valuable amendments to ministerial measures. The main theme of the radical peer was, however, that there was no such thing as parliamentary supremacy; that power rested with the people; and while Burke might hold firm to his expressed belief in the divine origin of government, he himself preferred to seek those natural causes which established constitutions upon a basis of consent. "The right is therefore fiduciary, the power limited.... Where is the difference," Abingdon asked, "between the despotism of the king of France, and the despotism of the parliament of England? And what is this but to erect an aristocratic tyranny in the state?" As for the colonists, the authority of their fellow subjects in England had always been limited and had now been disowned; but the Americans acknowledged the authority of the king; and if England feared that royal power would be increased by grants of money to him, let her provide for parliamentary control over the expenditure of this revenue. Abingdon dismissed with contempt the ministerial argument that, by insisting upon their direct responsibility to the crown, the colonies were fighting for arbitrary power at the same time that they were fighting for their liberties.

Although Lord Abingdon was the most ardent of antiministerialists, his pamphlet, with the controversies it revived, was of more consequence in accentuating whig divisions than in belaboring the government. "I am only afraid," Burke wrote to him, "that this kind of controversy will tend to confirm the people at large in an opinion (not at all as well founded as it is commonly thought) that there are unpleasant discussions, and great jealousies and animosities amongst ourselves."[110]

During the summer and autumn months between the parliamentary sessions of 1777, the whig leaders were convinced that they were powerless to interfere with the course of events determined by the ministry; they opened their minds to one another, and the real situation reveals itself. Charles Fox departed for a holiday in Ireland and, as he left, he wrote to Burke that no event was likely to happen which could serve their purpose. The influential members of Rockingham's little band, he continued, were "very pleasant and very amiable people; but altogether as unfit to storm a citadel, as they would be proper for the defence of it."[111] Fox here put his finger on the true nature of whig aristocracy at its best; and Burke, in a long and masterly reply, agreed with him that the defects he alluded to, though almost virtues in their magnanimity, were characteristic of "honest, disinterested intentions, plentiful fortunes, assured rank, and quiet homes." It was, he added, more surprising that Lord Rockingham, with his various handicaps, had persevered so long than that he grew languid and despondent at times. Moreover, even the people at large had shown a strange aversion to the whig cause, and preferred the more energetic banner of reviving toryism, which Archbishop Markham had recently upheld in a sermon calculated to intimidate the dissenters, the main bloc supporting the whig leaders.[112] Thus, Burke concluded, considering the people, the temper of whig leadership, and the necessities of war, "we must quietly give up all ideas of any settled, preconcerted plan."[113]

The inaction which even Burke accepted was less pleasing to some of his friends; and a few weeks later William Baker wrote anxiously for news of some plan of campaign. The irresolution of the whigs, he declared, had been such that even appearances had not been saved,

---

[110] *Correspondence*, II:176.

[111] *Correspondence of Edmund Burke*, II:182.

[112] *A Sermon Preached Before the Incorporated Society for the Propagation of the Gospel in Foreign Parts* (London, 1777).

[113] *Letter to the Hon. Charles James Fox* (Oct. 8, 1777). There is an interesting resemblance between this defense of the whig aristocracy and an impassioned outburst two years later from William Burke to the Duke of Portland, in which the writer wishes that the whigs had ambition or avarice or some other vice which would stir them to action. (Turberville, *op. cit.*, II:143–144.)

and any merit in opposition had been claimed by others. It was not enough for the whigs to cry out that parliament was corrupted, the king deceived, and the people abused. "We have waited too long in expectation of opportunities for action; they are in part made to our hands." Baker feared that it was almost hopeless "to reason men out of so inveterate a despondency as I perceive has seized some of the best amongst us"; but at least, he urged, there must be no slackening in concerted measures of resistance to the last ditch."[114] Burke passed on the tenor of such appeals to his leader, suggesting that at least there should be an appearance of activity, to counteract the malignant efforts of those who were trying with some success to infuse a sense of paralyzing languor into the whig leader. "I would," he added, referring to Rockingham's expressed opinion, "have the temporizing which I know to be necessary, rather evident to others, than proposed by you; and that it should seem the result of prudence, rather than of complexion. Let people stand still, but let them stop themselves rather by the great dyke before them than your bridle."[115]

The Duke of Richmond had also forgotten his languor, and was now urging Rockingham to prepare a definite plan of parliamentary opposition. Secession, he said, had failed, rightly or wrongly, and should be abandoned, despite Burke's recent defense of it as a policy. Moreover, it was not unlikely that news might come of an American victory; the whigs should be ready. Even without that, the accumulating burdens of war would lend increasing strength to the arguments of a persistent and straightforward opposition. The crusade against the influence of the crown should be constantly pushed, so that when the time came for a successful entry into power, that issue might be the means of undertaking it.[116]

In the latter half of November, 1777, the prospects and outlook of opposition changed so radically that it is not easy to find an adequate explanation, unless the mere fact of Chatham's recovery were responsible, together with the approach of a new parliamentary session. On November 15, Sir George Savile was still writing despondingly of the peculiar paralysis which invariably affected one group in opposition as

---

[114] *Correspondence of Edmund Burke*, II:187–192.
[115] *Ibid.*, pp. 198–201.
[116] Albemarle, *op. cit.*, II:315–319.

soon as another had summoned enough energy to attack, "a mortifying as well as ridiculous addition to the case being that the whole body of the patient, were it to unite its vigour, couldn't kill a mouse."[117] But on the 28th Thomas Townshend recorded his opinion that he "never saw so fair, or I may say a fair prospect of union among those in opposition till now. The only emulation seems to be, who shall be most accommodating to the general plan";[118] and the next day Fox wrote: "I am clear that the opinion of the majority of the house is now with us."[119] Chatham resumed correspondence with Rockingham with the theme of "All must unite"; and a meeting of the two groups on November 29 resulted in a reconciliation.[120] Three days later the news of Saratoga arrived.

It was soon clear that the whig reconciliation was one of personalities rather than of opinions, and instead of cementing the union, the American victory over Burgoyne served to weaken it, by raising once more the question of English authority over the colonies. On this point, ironically enough, while the whigs still differed from Chatham, they now differed in the opposite direction. Earlier quarrels had been over the Declaratory Act, and its assertion of complete legislative supremacy, which Chatham had opposed. By now the prospects of this legislative supremacy were becoming remote, and the followers of Rockingham and Burke were gradually reconciling themselves to American independence rather than an imperial connection which depended solely on the crown. Chatham on the other hand, thinking in terms of the empire which he had done so much to build, would "as soon subscribe to transubstantiation as to sovereignty (by right) in the colonies";[121] and for the rest of his life this was the stumbling block which thwarted the high whig hopes.

There can be little doubt that in the weeks following the news of Saratoga, many English political leaders changed their ideas on the question of American independence. Already in the few days of the parliamentary session which remained before the adjournment on

---

[117] *Ibid.*, II:321–324.
[118] Historical MSS Commission, 14th Rept., App. I (MSS of the Duke of Rutland), III:11.
[119] Russell, *Memorials and Correspondence of Charles James Fox*, I:159.
[120] *Correspondence of William Pitt*, IV:450–464; Albemarle, *op. cit.*, II:324–325.
[121] Lord Fitzmaurice, *Life of William, Earl of Shelburne* (London, 1912), II:10.

December 11 the more extreme followers of Rockingham declared themselves. In the Lords the Duke of Richmond declared that no terms could be made with America unless they included the recognition of independence; refusal to make the concession was a ridiculous and dangerous punctilio.[122] In the lower house David Hartley had given his opinion six months before that "a federal alliance was the only safe plan"; and he now remarked that he "did not see the horrors attending the legislative independence of your colonies that many people do."[123] The issue was not so clear-cut as it appears today, and when Hartley and others spoke of independence they probably had in mind some federal arrangement short of independent sovereignty. Some, like Fox, would have made independence the basis of free discussion with America in the hope of a federal alliance; others, like Burke, were for as much subordination as the colonies would accept. Nevertheless, such representative whigs were the pioneers of a shift in opinion which rapidly became more general, and by March, 1778, Thomas Hutchinson wrote that "never was such an instantaneous conversion of a whole kingdom."[124]

Chatham strenuously resisted the extreme implications of independence. In his speeches he emphasized the importance of the English connection with America, and he insisted upon this connection as the basis for any proposals of peace. Shelburne supported him, and noted with surprise how many people were going over to the opposite opinion.[125] Rockingham was evidently among the number; and when Chatham refused to modify his stand, the whig leader replied that America would never consent to a revival of English authority on that continent. Chatham replied coldly that further discussion would be fruitless. Once more the link had broken.[126]

This disagreement was of course well known to the ministry, and a serious attempt was made to utilize it. The news of Burgoyne's surrender had given the signal for a complete reconsideration of min-

[122] *Parliamentary History*, XIX:608.
[123] G. H. Guttridge, *David Hartley, M.P., an Advocate of Conciliation, 1774–1783*, Univ. Calif. Publ. Hist., XIV (1926):258–259; *Parliamentary History*, XVIII:259–260, 555.
[124] *Diary and Letters*, II:194.
[125] *Correspondence of William Pitt*, IV:480.
[126] *Ibid.*, pp. 489–492.

isterial policy. The morning after it arrived, Lord George Germain wrote anxiously to William Eden asking whether Lord North had slept at all, or had thought of any expedient for extricating the country out of its distresses. He went on to suggest that a drastic change of plan might be necessary.[127] "The consequences of this most fatal event," wrote North himself, "may be very important and serious and will certainly require some material change of system. No time shall be lost and no person who can give good information left unconsulted in the present moment."[128] During December, January, and February the government sought and received many memoranda suggesting all manner of schemes for war, for conciliation, and for the reorganization of the ministry.[129]

Under the changed circumstances, it was inevitable that Chatham's return to office should be considered. Rumors were soon afloat that he would come into power, and tentative approaches were made.[130] North asked to be replaced by a first minister less fettered by the past, but the king would not hear of his resignation, and was confirmed in his refusal by the news of Chatham's disagreement with Rockingham on American independence. North, he wrote, could now introduce his new policy at a fortunate time, with the opposition discredited and divided.[131] Chatham's breach with the whigs also lent color to the rumor that he would come into office. Bute and Mansfield were insistent that he should be sent for, and for several weeks he was the center of intrigue,[132] while from the whig side Richmond took it upon himself to heal the breach and reunite the opposition. If, he wrote, Chatham could see any practical possibility of keeping the empire intact, he (Richmond) would support him.[133]

[127] Auckland MSS (Brit. Mus.), III, fol. 394.

[128] *Correspondence of King George III*, III, No. 2095.

[129] "Adam Smith on the American Revolution: An Unpublished Memorial," *Am. Hist. Rev.*, XXXVIII: 714–720; *Private Papers of John, Earl of Sandwich* (Navy Records Society, 1932), I:323 ff.; Auckland MSS, III, fol. 395 (William Eden to Lord North, Dec. 7, 1777).

[130] Vergennes to Gérard (B. F. Stevens, *Facsimiles*, No. 786; see also No. 1814); Russell, *Memorials and Correspondence of Charles James Fox*, I:166; Auckland MSS, IV, fol. 100; *Correspondence of William Pitt*, IV:485–486.

[131] *Correspondence of King George III*, IV, Nos. 2179, 2184.

[132] *Correspondence of William Pitt*, IV:493–497; *Diary and Letters of Thomas Hutchinson*, II:183; E. H. Coleridge, *Life of Thomas Coutts* (London, 1920), I, chap. 6.

[133] *Correspondence of William Pitt*, IV:498–499.

About the middle of March definite negotiations to bring Chatham into office were begun by William Eden.[184] He proposed that North should remain as first lord of the treasury and chancellor of the exchequer, Chatham having "honours" and a place in the cabinet, with Shelburne as secretary of state, and offices for Dunning, Barré, and Fox. This was a step clearly designed to get the support of Chatham and those in opposition who were not immediately attached to Rockingham. As North wrote to the king, they would be more reasonable than the Rockingham group, more attentive to the dignity of the crown, and more able to give prestige without too many encumbrances. The king, who was not sanguine, agreed, stipulating only that North must remain at the head and must be the intermediary between himself and Chatham.[185]

Eden began his operations by visiting Charles Fox, and thence through Dr. Priestley he approached Shelburne. Shelburne took the firm stand that "Lord Chatham must be the dictator," and this, he said, meant a change considerable enough to annihilate every party in the kingdom. Grafton and Rockingham must be included, Gower and Germain dismissed, and Mansfield's influence ended. The king, however, insisted on retaining most of his henchmen except Germain, his idea apparently being to replace Germain by Chatham in the office most concerned with American administration; but he refused to see Chatham until the appointments to the cabinet had been made.[186]

At this point, news of the American alliance with France was confirmed, and a meeting of the leaders of opposition was held. Rockingham stood up stoutly for recognizing American independence to prevent war with France, which, as they rightly anticipated, Chatham would hotly demand. Shelburne, for Chatham, would not accept this policy, and the opposition remained as far divided as ever.[187]

North was now beseeching the king to yield to Chatham, whose demands were the lowest, before the opposition increased its terms. Chatham, he said, would be more reasonable now than a fortnight

---

[184] *Correspondence of King George III*, IV, Nos. 2219–2221; Russell, *Memorials and Correspondence of Charles James Fox*, I:180; Fitzmaurice, *Life of Shelburne*, II:15 ff.
[185] *Correspondence of King George III*, IV, No. 2221.
[186] *Ibid.*, Nos. 2223–2224.
[187] Albemarle, *op. cit.*, II:347 ff.

hence.[138] The king was adamant. "It is not private pique," he replied, "but an opinion formed on an experience of a reign of now seventeen years that makes me resolve to run any personal risk rather than submit to opposition. . . and the road opened to a set of men who certainly would make me a slave for the remainder of my days."[139] One may note that, only a few weeks before, Richmond had declared to Rockingham that the whigs should not undertake an administration if there was to be "only a suspension of evils," and if they were not allowed to eradicate the cause, the overgrown influence of the crown.[140] The issue is quite plain. The king would accept members of opposition in the existing ministry, but would not yield power completely to any of them.

The grounds of negotiation were being circulated among the well-informed in political society. Horace Walpole expressed the opinion that no one willing to serve with North could be found among the opposition, except possibly Chatham and Shelburne.[141] North tried to force the king's hand by reporting that the opposition, still unable to agree among themselves, had decided to submit unreservedly to Chatham's leadership, and had sent Lord Granby to Hayes with this message. The king would not budge an inch. "I am extremely indifferent," he wrote, "whether Lord Granby goes or does not go with the abject message of the Rockingham party this day to Hayes; I will certainly send none to that place"; and he proceeded to inquire about other possible changes to strengthen the existing ministry.[142]

North continued his agonized plea for Chatham, who, he said, would soon be no longer content with control of the chief offices, but would demand a universal change. On March 29 he prophesied that Chatham's forthcoming visit to the House of Lords would produce a firm union with Rockingham, and he repeated the former arguments. The nation, he went on, did not think ill of the integrity of the present ministers, but was beginning to think indifferently of their judgment. Once more the king expressed his displeasure, and asked North for explicit answers to three questions: Could the present

---

[138] *Correspondence of King George III*, IV, Nos. 2225, 2228.
[139] *Ibid.*, No. 2226.   [141] *Last Journals* (1859), II:237.
[140] Albemarle, *op. cit.*, II:318.   [142] *Correspondence of King George III*, IV, No. 2240.

administration be strengthened from opposition? If not, would North help to revive vigor everywhere? Or, failing that, would he at least serve until the end of the session? North agreed to continue for the time, but he could give no assurance on the first two heads, and by now the king was seeking advice from Lord Weymouth.[143]

Early in April, Chatham appeared in London. The Rockingham whigs had prepared a motion for withdrawing the troops from America, and in their anxiety to win Chatham's support they consulted Shelburne and made all the changes he thought necessary. It was in vain; and on April 7 Chatham appealed to his fellow peers to resist the whig proposals and refuse independence to America. He appealed for his ideal of empire unbroken—as if that were possible—and in the act of speaking was stricken down, to linger but a few weeks.[144] The following evening George III wrote to his unwilling minister, "May not the political exit of Lord Chatham incline you to continue at the head of my affairs?"[145]

---

[143] *Correspondence of King George III,* IV, Nos. 2255–2256.
[144] *Parliamentary History,* XIX:1012 ff.
[145] *Correspondence of King George III,* IV, No. 2284.

IV. THE ATTACK ON THE MINISTRY

AFTER Saratoga the problem of reconstruction was less embarrassing to the whigs, for it was apparent that American independence must come. In fact, the whigs accepted the prospect of independence with an alacrity that would be surprising were it not for their fear of the crown. For them it must be parliamentary supremacy or nothing. They had no love for an imperial connection through the king alone, and when Lord North appointed a commission to go to America with conciliatory proposals on this basis, the whigs came out strongly in an opposition now at last on congenial ground. Lord North's proposals, said Burke, would increase the prerogative as they diminished the empire. The commissioners would surrender everything but the power and patronage of the crown. W. S. Stanhope came still nearer home when he said, "The high tone of prerogative and supremacy will cease there, as it has done here, and in its room the milder voice of influence will be heard."[1]

Such comments launched the attack that was to continue for the rest of the war. Several years earlier, the Bishop of St. Asaph had attacked the penal laws for their tendency to establish the power of governing America by influence and corruption; Richard Champion had declared that an American revenue would be used only to strengthen the enormous power of the crown through placemen and pensioners; and James Burgh, in his popular *Political Disquisitions*, had gone so far as to say that the ministry had caused the break with America "all to get a few more places for their wretched dependents."[2] So now in 1778 the conduct of that war was freely assailed as intended to increase royal power and no longer to preserve the authority of parliament and the regulation of trade. "The motives which I impute to them," wrote Hartley, "are a design to establish an influential dominion, to be exercised at the pleasure of the crown, and to acquire an independent revenue at the disposition of the crown, uncontrolled and not account-

---

[1] *Parliamentary History,* XIX:779, 798; XX:758.
[2] *A Speech Intended to Have Been Spoken* . . . (London, 1774), reprinted in P. Force, *American Archives,* 4th ser., I:97–104; Guttridge, *The American Correspondence of a Bristol Merchant,* Univ. Calif. Publ. Hist., XXII (1934):46; Burgh, *Political Disquisitions* (London, 1774), II:275.

able for to parliament."[3] "The crown wanted a revenue," wrote another pamphleteer, "to extend its own influence by feeding its needy dependents, to have thirteen custom houses, thirteen excise officers, thirteen stamp officers, thirteen post offices, with a variety of other posts and employments, and to devour America with the same train of vermin to which this country has been so long a prey."[4]

Moreover, the American war had brought into existence a formidable army under the control of the crown. Such an army would be a very proper instrument, said Fox, for effecting points of a greater, or more favorite importance nearer home—points perhaps very unfavorable to the liberties of this country.[5] The Duke of Richmond "dreaded the return of that army to these kingdoms. It may totally subvert the remains of freedom."[6] As for Burke, we have his assurance, restated several years later, that "he was strongly of the opinion that such armies, first victorious over Englishmen in a conflict for English constitutional rights and privileges and afterwards habituated to keep an English people in a state of subjection, would prove fatal in the end to the liberties of England itself."[7] Thus, in the name of liberty, ran the whig attack on the American war. Behind it all lay their hostility to the king.

The king could hardly be attacked directly; but Burke had already shown the way by his allegations of secret advisers and an inner cabinet, and early in the war he continued the campaign by referring to Charles Jenkinson as the real minister.[8] Similar charges were directed toward Lord Mansfield "sitting in silence behind the curtain ... guiding the political machine."[9] The more cautious referred to "unconstitutional control and advice," but others came near the real object. Ministers were but "puppets in office, moved from behind the curtain": and an essential for new ministers was their independence of "the invisible power," which must be dragged into the light of day.[10]

---

[3] David Hartley, *Letters on the American War* (London, 1778), p. 41.
[4] *A Letter to the Whigs* (London, 1779), p. 18.
[5] *Parliamentary History*, XVIII:1431.
[6] *Ibid.*, XIX:404.
[7] *Appeal from the New to the Old Whigs.*
[8] *Parliamentary History*, XVIII:895.
[9] *The Plea of the Colonies* (London, 1776).
[10] *Parliamentary History*, XX:1029; XIX:917.

Another form of oblique attack praised the king's private virtues and found it impossible to attribute to him "the fatal career which had brought the crown and empire to the verge of ruin; there must therefore be some invisible hand that secretly moved all these counsels."[11] These attacks were of course aimed at the king himself, and differed only in outward politeness from the more impudent phraseology of Lord Abingdon, who moved an amendment to the address with the phrase, "Awakened as your majesty must at length be to the impending ruin of the state."[12]

The whigs, however, did not have the argument all their way. The king used a formidable weapon against them when he truly said of the American war, "I am fighting the battle of the legislature, therefore have a right to expect an almost unanimous support."[13] Lord North was a great parliamentarian, and from the beginning to the end of the war he met the whigs on their own ground. As early as 1770 he had used this argument against his critics. "The language of America," he said, "is, We are the subjects of the king; with parliament we have nothing to do."[14] The ministry, he said in 1775, "contended for the rights of parliament, while the Americans talked of their belonging to the crown. Their language therefore was that of toryism."[15] The whig opposition, wrote Archbishop Markham, "used their best endeavours to throw the whole weight and power of the colonies into the scale of the crown; . . . they have maintained that a king of England has the power to discharge any number of his subjects . . . from the allegiance that is due to the state."[16] And as late as 1781 North gave a reasoned defense of the ministry on the same ground.[17]

It was possible to appeal to many varieties of support against the whig attack. To some, though not the most farsighted, the proprietary notion of "our colonies" still operated to discredit any weakening of control. "If they are free from parliament," declared one pamphleteer,

---

[11] *Ibid.*, XIX:1307.

[12] *Ibid.*, XX:880.

[13] *The Correspondence of King George III*, ed. Sir John Fortescue (London, 1928), III, No. 1709.

[14] *Sir Henry Cavendish's Debates* (London, 1841), II:31.

[15] *Parliamentary History*, XVIII:771.

[16] *A Sermon Preached Before the Incorporated Society for the Propagation of the Gospel in Foreign Parts* (London, 1777).

[17] *Parliamentary History*, XXII:715–717.

"there is no power to ensure submission to the crown. The colonies are the public dominions of the realm, not the private patrimony of the prince."[18] This demand for authority merged into an insistence on the rule of law, failing which the imperial relationship would dissolve in chaos.

But there were difficulties of a higher order than these. When Shelburne spoke of virtual self-government in America, or when Hartley advocated a "federal union," the legal mind found it difficult to grapple with the fact of a division of sovereignty within the empire. In the critical days after Saratoga, Shelburne advocated for America "not a corrupt or slavish dependency, calculated to enlarge the influence of the crown, . . . but a fair, honest, wise and honourable connection, in which the constitutional prerogatives of the crown, the claims of parliament, and the liberties, properties, and lives of all the subjects of the British empire would be equally secured." But, objected Lord Chancellor Thurlow, "if America were to have a legislative power, competent to every act of sovereignty, then . . . here would be two sovereignties";[19] and such an apparent impossibility stuck in the throat of many a constitutionally minded Englishman. Burke and his noble colleagues were forced to avoid this constitutional obstacle if they could, but their cautious efforts to obtain a practical autonomy for America without the appearance of a separate sovereignty or royal aggrandizement weakened their own vigor without gaining support from the other side, which deliberately included whigs and radicals in one sweeping condemnation.

The conservative and backward-looking whigs were always particularly sensitive to the charge of factious conduct. It was not long since the idea of organized opposition had been regarded as unpatriotic. Chatham and Shelburne had their own reasons for retaining much of this attitude, and the whig dukes felt the accusation keenly. It was thus a favorite weapon with their opponents. "It is objected to the present ministry," said Dundas in 1779, "that they depend for their existence solely on the influence of the crown and that of their adherents in this house; that they have not a great party on their side,

---

[18] *A Short Appeal to the People of Great Britain* (London, 1776).
[19] *Parliamentary History*, XX:36–41.

consisting of the great families of the country. . . . If I thought that they kept their places by the strength of a faction of this kind, I would vote for their removal tomorrow."[20] "A party spirit," said one pamphleteer, whose words found echo in many more, "is the hereditary curse of British politics."[21] Organized opposition was still genuinely distasteful to many, not only to the officeholders; although even they sometimes, like Lord Barrington, clung to office partly out of sheer loyalty, long after its rewards had ceased to ease their minds."[22]

In the earlier years of the war the opposition had found it impossible to overcome the ministerial advantage which came from the apparent necessity of a coercive policy. When France came in, the whigs, who were second to none in their hostility to the great power across the channel, were caught in the meshes of the dual struggle, and their advocacy of peace with America for the sake of war with France did not tempt a large following. But as the disaster of Saratoga was followed by manifest incompetence in the war with France, ministerial supporters weakened in their allegiance. There was still no eagerness to accept the lead of opposition. There was, however, a better opportunity for an attack on the government than there had been since the war began, if only the whigs would not insist on their theoretical principles but would simply attack the conduct of the war. "It has been acknowledged," wrote a pamphleteer of 1778, "by the most sanguine-minded among them, that the defence of American liberty was unpopular (Mr. Fox has again and again allowed that the American question was unpopular) yet they have uniformly persevered in declaiming in favour of that liberty; and while the torrent of popular rage was ready at every moment to burst out against our ministers for their ill-conduct, the people could repose no confidence in the minority, whose principles they abhorred. . . . Had the importance of the names of Wentworth and Cavendish, aided by the abilities of a Fox and a Burke, overlooked the abstract question of American taxation and considered merely the conduct of the war; had they thought means, perhaps not perfectly consistent with their opinion, justifiably used in removing men whose conduct they deemed hurtful to the

---

[20] *Ibid.*, XX:1240.
[21] *A Letter to the King from an Old Patriotic Quaker* (London, 1778), p. 118.
[22] *The Political Life of William Wildman, Viscount Barrington* (London, 1815).

constitution; they might before this time have given a final blow to the power of an irresolute and unsuccessful administration."[23]

In the first half of 1779 the ministerial conduct of the war became the subject of acute public dissatisfaction. Parliamentary inquiries were initiated into the conduct of the American campaigns under the Howes and Burgoyne. The indecisive naval action off Ushant was followed by courts-martial on Admirals Keppel and Palliser. In all these investigations the issue of responsibility lay between the commanders and the government. It was necessary for Sandwich at the admiralty and Germain as secretary of state to justify themselves at the expense of their chosen officers, and since the leading officers were whig in sympathy the controversies became partisan. The opposition attempted to place all the blame on the ministry, especially on Sandwich and Germain, and could muster wide public support in criticism of ministerial inefficiency.

The complicated story of the Battle of Ushant contains all the elements of administrative incompetence, naval inefficiency, and political jealousy. Keppel was an admiral whose promotion had been made easy by his high whig birth and aristocratic connections. Palliser represented the changes in favor introduced by the new reign. Older than Keppel but junior in rank, he was advanced by Sandwich to positions of influence which gave him an advantage over Keppel, his superior on active service. The disagreement between the two, when in actual contact with the French fleet, became an issue of ministry versus opposition. The court-martial and acquittal of Keppel was the signal for ardent partisan and political demonstrations against the ministry. The resignation of Palliser was followed by the compensation of a lucrative place in the gift of the crown. The merits and demerits of either side cannot be exactly estimated,[24] but the ministry could not pass such continuous scrutiny without exposing its manifest shortcomings. More and more it appeared that patronage was maintaining incompetence in the conduct of the war.

---

[23] *An Examination into the Conduct of the Present Administration* (London, 1778), p. 6.

[24] *Life of Augustus, Viscount Keppel* (London, 1842), II; *Private Papers of John, Earl of Sandwich* (Navy Records Society, 1933), II; W. M. James, *The British Navy in Adversity* (London, 1933).

On the other hand, the violence of partisan denunciations gave no sure guarantee of a better alternative. Independent members of parliament were dissatisfied with the ministry; but they were equally suspicious of faction. "Happily for the ministry," observed Barrington, "the opposition is so universally detested and feared that they find a support in the nation to which they are not entitled but from *comparison*."[25] "It was the wish of Great Britain," wrote Sir Gilbert Elliot three years later, "to recover America. Government aimed at least at this object, which the opposition rejected. Those therefore who thought the war with America just and practicable, however much they may be dissatisfied with the abilities of the ministers, or disgusted with their mismanagements or misfortunes, had yet no choice left them. . . . This I take to have been the true bond between parliament and the late ministry, and the true key to its otherwise unaccountable longevity."[26]

It was remarked by the more penetrating critics that a peculiar feature of the American war was the degree in which parliament had been asked to authorize ministerial measures. As early as 1775, Lord Shelburne had objected in the House of Lords "to the current ministerial language that parliament did this and parliament did that, for he insisted that parliament had done nothing; it was the ministry had done all";[27] and Burke had insisted that the whole force of whig strategy must be directed to prevent the participation of parliament in the ministerial policy of coercion. That strategy had failed by 1776, and the ministerial majority had carried all before it, while the whigs in despair went to the length of secession. "The minister has had address enough to make every measure of ordinary execution a measure of legislation," said one pamphleteer.[28] Every American measure, wrote another, is supposed to need parliamentary sanction; ministerial responsibility is diminished, and the war suffers inefficiency and delay.[29] Lord North, when hard pressed in 1780, used this excuse to meet the charge of ministerial influence. With regard to the American

[25] Historical MSS Commission, 17th Rept., Lothian MSS, p. 351.
[26] *Life and Letters of Sir Gilbert Elliot*, ed. Countess of Minto, I:76.
[27] *Parliamentary History*, XVIII:449.
[28] *An Examination into the Conduct of the Present Administration* (London, 1778).
[29] *A Speech on Some Political Topics* (London, 1779), pp. 26–27, 39.

war, he said, and the various measures pursued relative to it, they were not his measures as a minister; they were all grounded on acts of the legislature. In proposing and consenting to those bills, he had acted as a member of parliament, and as such only was responsible.[30] Bishop Watson summed up the whig dilemma when he wrote: "The mischief of the American war was carried on under the sanction of parliament, and every other mischief will be carried on in the same way: for a minister would want common sense to run any risk in taking upon himself responsibility for obnoxious measures, when he could secure the consent of parliament to almost any measure he might propose. I see not in the nature of our government any remedy for this evil."[31]

The whigs, however, did see a remedy in the reduction of royal patronage. By 1779 the war had become unpopular enough to arouse another wave of agitation not unlike that of ten years earlier; and again, cautiously and tentatively, Rockingham and his friends blessed the movement, provided it did not go too far.

In the last few weeks of 1779, as the parliamentary session approached, the growing anxiety of the electorate began to appear in the same form which it had taken ten years earlier, that is, in meetings and petitions from counties and boroughs. Many of the same persons were concerned as in 1769, and the precedent was recognized. In the previous wave of agitation over the Middlesex election the issue had been mainly constitutional. The rights of electors had been outraged by the arbitrary action of the House of Commons in declaring a candidate with fewer votes than John Wilkes the duly elected member for the county of Middlesex. The contest had been, in the phrase of the petitioners from Yorkshire, a contest of the representation of the people in opposition to the people; and "the people" meant in practice the restricted electorate of property.[32] Meetings of the electors had been held, and petitions for redress presented to the crown.

In supporting the movement to petition the crown, whig leaders had insisted that there must be a demand only for the dissolution of parliament, not for constitutional changes. Thus the existing electorate might once more assume the decision by returning the members of

---

[30] *Parliamentary History,* XXI:363.
[31] *Anecdotes of the Life of Richard Watson* (London, 1817), p. 84.
[32] *Wyvill Papers,* I:xix.

its choice. The injured county of Middlesex ignored this request, but others observed it, notably the electors of Yorkshire, where the influence of Lord Rockingham and his friends was especially great. When the petitions brought no result, the freeholders had been at a loss what to do next. In Yorkshire they had rejected the suggestion of a further remonstrance and a committee to see it carried out, and had contented themselves with expressing their indignation to the members of parliament for the county. Parliamentary action proved ineffective, and the North ministry clung precariously to power until the force of electoral wrath spent itself and the division among leaders of opposition produced the expected failure. The moderation of the Rockingham group offset the more aggressive leadership of Chatham, and Lord North rode out the storm.

Now in 1779 the situation was not dissimilar, although the grievances were less related to constitutional rights than to maladministration. The American war was a failure, and the hope of easier taxation had gone. The expenses of the war were mounting, and the incompetence of the ministry drew attention to its system of influence. Lord North had been reduced to a pitiable state of indecision; "the most altered man I ever saw in my life," wrote Robinson, "he has not spirits to set to anything." "Nothing can be more miserable than I am," the unhappy minister declared.[33] There were defections from the ministry, and intrigues within it. Lord Gower resigned, declaring that his resignation was not prompted by any sympathies for opposition, who were more wicked than administration was weak.[34] The king's agents vainly set about negotiations to strengthen the ministry. They gathered that the more accessible leaders of opposition, Camden, Grafton, and Shelburne, were still against American independence, but would not serve with North, Sandwich, and Germain.[35] Thus there seemed to be the unsatisfactory possibility of exchanging one trio of ministers for another, with but a problematical increase of strength. Charles Jenkinson, the new secretary at war, approved of a negotiation with the opposition; for, he argued, even if they insisted on including the Rockingham whigs, the two would soon quarrel and leave the way again

---

[33] Add. MSS (Brit. Mus.) 38,212 (Liverpool Papers, XXIII), fol. 56; *Correspondence of King George III*, IV, Nos. 2851, 2857.
[34] *Ibid.*, No. 2777.　　　[35] *Ibid.*, No. 2823.

open to royal decision. It would be wise, he wrote to the king, to make it clear that the whigs were not personally unwelcome to him.[36] Meanwhile, government was carried on only by the combined efforts of the king, Jenkinson, and John Robinson, the senior secretary of the treasury.[37] These three endeavored to keep North in motion; and even though their efforts were in the main friendly to him, they took on the nature of an intrigue, during which the relation of Robinson and Jenkinson with the king often seemed closer than that of North himself. This situation could not be accurately known at the time to those outside the intimate circle, but it gives some justification for the rumors and accusations of that secret influence and inner cabinet which Burke had denounced in 1770.

It was easy now for critics to assail and magnify the extravagance of a patronage which merely insured the stability of an unsuccessful administration. The merchants could expect nothing from a continuation of the war, and the country gentlemen were particularly susceptible to appeals directed against a profligate and incompetent ministry entrenched in a complacent House of Commons. The parliamentary session opened in November, 1779, and the opposition immediately began its campaign against the waste of public money on a policy which had brought the country to a state which they delighted to contrast with the prosperity and prestige of 1760. The campaign in parliament was waged with increased vigor and ability, and it accompanied a significant onslaught by influential sections of the electorate, chiefly from the counties.

At first the new movement in the counties followed closely the precedent of 1769. In Yorkshire a few gentlemen from the North Riding, headed by Christopher Wyvill, proposed to summon a meeting of the freeholders of the county, and sounded the potential supporters of such a meeting. The object would be to petition the House of Commons for an inquiry into the civil list, pensions, and places. From that beginning it might be possible to work for the effective freedom of parliament.[38] Many of those consulted expressed both sympathy and

---

[36] *Correspondence of King George III*, IV, Nos. 2825, 2828.

[37] H. Butterfield, "Lord North and Mr. Robinson, 1779," *Cambridge Historical Journal*, V(1937):255–279.

[38] *Wyvill Papers*, III:107 ff.

pessimism; but it was soon clear that, once started, the movement would gather strength. One or two influential and courageous gentlemen came forward less equivocally, and by the second week in December the meeting was being planned. Supporters of the ministry tried to brand the proposal as partisan, but its organizers determined to steer clear of the dangerous shoals of faction. In this they were upheld by Sir George Savile, member of parliament for Yorkshire and, according to John Lee, the sole county member who could not be turned out by a concerted ministerial drive. Savile had been a despondent friend of opposition throughout its long exile, taking the view that the whigs could do little more than wait until a general uprising of the electorate should change the ministerial system. Now that such an uprising seemed possible, he advised its promoters to do without the leadership of party. "If the country feel," he said, "the country must speak."[39]

Many opinions were set forth in this preliminary correspondence, but it was clear that the most complete union of all those who opposed the government was needed for any hope of success. The reformers must rally also the conservatives, who, in the words of Charles Turner, had "thus far considered the emoluments and patronage of the country as due wages for having banished the Stuarts and arbitrary power."[40] In the expectation of this whig support the meeting of freeholders took place on December 30.

The ministry watched the preparations with concern. John Robinson, secretary to the treasury, called together about ten Yorkshire peers and gentlemen who supported the government, and it was their unanimous opinion that they had better not attend the meeting, but privately discourage it, and if necessary protest against it.[41] Thus there was no effective ministerial minority when the freeholders met at York. The only spokesman for the unpopular side was Leonard Smelt, who took high royal ground and attacked the whig administrations of the past. On the other side there appeared a formidable array of the great whig nobility and gentry, the Dukes of Devonshire and Rutland, Rockingham himself, the Cavendishes, the members for the county

---

[39] *Ibid.*, pp. 153–157.   [40] *Ibid.*, p. 170.
[41] Add. MSS, 38,212 (Liverpool Papers, XXIII), fol. 316; Auckland MSS, V, fol. 489.

and the city of York, and many other influential persons to make up a company "within the compass of a single room, who possessed landed property to the amount of eight hundred thousand pounds per annum"—more property, as Sir George Savile later pointed out, than within the walls of the House of Commons itself.[42]

Wyvill was at pains to explain that the meeting was not partisan and that Rockingham was not responsible for it, but that it originated with private country gentlemen "totally free from all party influence." The resolutions proposed, first, a petition to the House of Commons asking for administrative and financial reform before the imposition of new burdens, and, second, the setting up of a committee of association to further the aims of the petition. There was some latitude in the wording of the resolutions, which were obviously designed to include the full range of opinion expressed at the meeting, from the conservatively skeptical to the radical reformers. The conservatives predominated in influence, and possibly in numbers, and there was no specific mention of reform in the constitution of parliament.[43]

Already, while preparations had been proceeding for the meeting at York, the county of Middlesex had been considering the same kind of action. Late in December, John Jebb addressed a pamphlet to a meeting of the Middlesex freeholders, who had recently presented a petition to parliament on a specific electoral grievance. In this address Jebb alluded to the forthcoming county meetings and laid down proposals for the systematic organization of a national convention composed of delegates from the county electors in proportion to their respective numbers. Such a convention, he said, representing the electorate directly, would have greater authority than the House of Commons itself, and could, if it wished, even declare the dissolution of that house. Such ideas closely resembled the radical program of Major Cartwright; but even Jebb did not commit himself to the theory of popular representation. "The interests of all classes and descriptions of men should, without respect of parties, be effectually consulted.... Whether these interests may be best secured by attending to property or to numbers, is a subject deserving of the most serious attention."[44]

---

[42] *Parliamentary History*, XX:1376.   [43] *Wyvill Papers*, I:9–40.
[44] *Works . . . of John Jebb* (London, 1787), II:453 ff.

In fact, when the freeholders of Middlesex met on January 7, they avowedly followed the moderate lead of Yorkshire. One gentleman suggested that the statement of grievances should be strengthened by a declaration that the American colonies had been driven to revolt by the conduct of administration, but he was persuaded to withdraw his amendment, and practically the same petition and plan for a committee of association were carried as at York. The Duke of Portland and three other whig peers were present.[45]

The conspicuous difference between the action of these meetings and those of 1769 lay in two matters: first, that the petitions were addressed to the House of Commons, not to the king, and were later to be presented there with effective emphasis; second, that the principle of association was adopted, according to which a continuous organization could further the expressed aims of the meetings by consulting in a general conference. This procedure seemed to some unduly aggressive. The American congress, they declared, was its archetype, and Dr. Price 'had introduced the idea into England.'[46] Nevertheless it marked a significant step toward national organization for reform, in an age when the country was so divided geographically that agitation on any question, good or bad, was likely to be confined to the localities directly concerned.

County meetings now spread rapidly throughout the country. Hertford and Huntingdon provided some controversy, for in both counties Lord Sandwich was able to bring ministerial pressure to bear, but petitions and committees were organized in each. Sussex, Surrey, Bedford, and Essex came next, and Lord North's own county of Somerset. By the end of January eighteen counties had met, and all but one, or possibly two, had adopted the petitions for economical reform. Nine more followed during February and March. Several towns also came in: York, London, Westminster, Nottingham, Reading, Gloucester, and Newcastle. Occasionally there was a desire to add recommendations for constitutional change, but union was preserved on the more moderate basis of administrative reform. Under the leadership of

---

[45] *The Remembrancer* (London, 1780), p. 106; *Wyvill Papers*, I:58–60.
[46] *Observations on an Address to the Freeholders of Middlesex* (London, 1780).

Wyvill the committees appointed by many of the meetings sent representatives to a conference which met in London during the second and third weeks of March. Thirteen counties and five towns were represented at this conference, of which the keynote was a violent attack on the "enormous, the compactly accumulated, the all-devouring influence of the crown. By an unhappy war with America, begotten in the first influence of this despotic system, and nursed with a view of giving completion to it, this fatal influence has been armed with more ample means than ever it enjoyed before, for enslaving parliament."[47] These were strong words; and already the rift was appearing between conservative and radical, for the conference went on to advocate measures of representational reform. For the time, however, the attack on influence was the common enterprise in parliament and out.

In the call for this conference the originating committees, determined to avoid the stigma of party, had requested the appointment of deputies who were not members of either house of parliament. This restriction caused some anxiety, and Wyvill agreed to accept a gentleman's agreement to make it unnecessary. "My objection," he wrote to Lord Mahon, of the Westminster committee, which had elected Charles Fox, "is not personally to Mr. Fox, but... to all great Partizans and Parliamentary leaders of either House.... The public is jealous of such men, and their interference in the most important business of the petitioners would give it an air of party, to which I must withhold my consent." In the interests of harmony and reform, therefore, prominent party men refrained from sitting in the meeting of deputies, and the ban on members of parliament as such was lifted.[48]

There was naturally a close connection between the activity of county meetings and the campaign of the opposition in parliament. When parliament met, on November 25, 1779, the whigs opened a systematic attack on ministerial extravagance and corruption; and this meant also an attack on patronage and influence. There was a more concentrated effort and a more definite plan of operations than had been usual since the war began. On December 7 the Duke of Richmond moved for the reform of the civil list; on the 9th the army

---

[47] Wyvill, *op. cit.*, I:120 ff., 429.   [48] *Ibid.*, III:180–181.

estimates were carried by only 159 votes to 113; and on the 15th Burke gave notice that he would introduce a plan of economical reform. "I never until lately," he said, "saw a temper in the least favourable to reformation. There is now a dawning of hope."[49] Shelburne also, defeated in an attempt to reduce expenses, gave notice of a motion for inquiry into expenditure, contracts, and the civil list. Both sections of opposition thus concentrated upon the vulnerable financial structure, which was also the key to ministerial control of parliament.

The same policy had been adopted by the county associations, and at first the uprising of the electorate gave added force to opposition. This was apparent in the large attendance of peers when Shelburne introduced his motion on February 8; and on the same day Sir George Savile presented the Yorkshire petition in the Commons. He was supported by petitions from York and Bristol, the latter presented by Burke, with whom Savile declared that he had had no consultation on the plan of economical reform, similar as it was to the petitions. Three days later Burke obtained leave to bring in the bill incorporating his plan. This bill reached the committee stage on March 8; and by then the effect of the county meetings was evident. Two lords lieutenant, including Lord Carmarthen for the county of Yorkshire, had been dismissed for participating in the meetings, and the full artillery of whig nobility was brought out in resentment of insults comparable only to the similar dismissals in the early years of the reign. Even the silent Duke of Devonshire was moved to speak in parliament. Rockingham himself, conspicuously reticent, became almost a frequent speaker. Moreover, on March 6 Lord North had introduced his budget, after expressing to the king his fears that the new taxes might "cause a great convulsion, and give so much weight to the petitions as to force the government to give way to opposition and their measures, especially if the people compare too nicely the advantages to result from the dependence of America and the evils to be apprehended from these additional burdens."[50]

In this atmosphere Burke's bill came into committee. The clause abolishing the third secretaryship of state was defeated by 208 votes

---

[49] *Parliamentary History*, XX:1299.
[50] *Correspondence of King George III*, V, No. 2959.

to 201. "You see," Earl Fitzwilliam wrote to the Yorkshire committee, "nothing can be done in parliament. You must take care of yourselves."[51] On March 13, however, the clause to abolish the board of trade was carried by 207 to 199. On the 20th the tide turned again, this time more perceptibly; a third clause, which touched the king's household, was defeated by more than fifty votes, and Burke declared his indifference to the fate of the remainder.[52] Nevertheless, the pressure from the constituencies persisted, and on the 6th of April John Dunning carried the motion which has made his name famous.

Dunning's motion, made in the committee of the whole House, on consideration of the petitions from county meetings, read, in its original form: "That it is the opinion of this committee, that the influence of the crown has increased, is increasing and ought to be diminished." A ministerial amendment, accepted by the proposer, inserted the words "that it is necessary to declare"; and in this form the motion was carried by 233 votes to 215. The rhythm of the motion caught the fancy of contemporaries, as it later attracted historians, and its significance has sometimes been misunderstood. It was a lawyer's motion, worded with care as well as with distinction, and it was directed ostensibly at ministerial patronage, not at royal power. So far as the king played a part in patronage and the determination of policy, he was inevitably concerned in the accusation; but there is no reason to doubt that the term "influence of the crown" was used in its strict political sense, the accumulation of parliamentary votes by patronage in the control of ministers. The king of course regarded the motion as an attack on himself. "The resolutions," he wrote, "can by no means be looked on as personal to [Lord North]; I wish I did not feel at whom they are *personally levelled*."[53]

The motion was followed by two others, the first declaring the competence of the House to inquire into all branches of public revenue, including the civil list, and the second expressing the obligation of the House to redress the abuses complained of in the petitions. Both

[51] *Wyvill Papers*, IV:129.

[52] *Parliamentary History*, XXI:296 ff.

[53] *Correspondence of King George III*, V, Nos. 2986–2987. It will be noted that if the term "influence of the crown" had meant "royal influence" in the vague modern sense, the king's comment would be pointless.

were carried without a division. Four days later, Dunning followed up these theoretical victories with resolutions providing for an annual statement of payments to members of parliament, and for the disqualification of thirteen specified placemen from such membership. The first resolution passed with the same ease as before, but the second was carried by a majority of only two votes; and in the discussion, Henry Dundas, the ministerial spokesman, quoted Burke's own attack on place bills against the motion.

The momentary success was soon over. "Things begin to wear a better aspect," the king wrote to North. "Several ... have been led on farther than they intended, and numbers will return; for it cannot be the wish of the majority to overturn the constitution."[54] Dunning had been taunted at the moment of triumph with the prophecy that his new friends would prove a rope of sand; and so it was. A bill to disfranchise revenue officers was defeated on the 13th, a contractors' bill the next day; and the climax came on the 24th, when Dunning's own motion that parliament should not be prorogued until the petitions had been acted upon was defeated by 254 votes to 203. This was a motion which seemed to restrict the royal prerogative of dissolution. Hitherto, in all the agitation against ministerial influence the prerogative had not been seriously challenged, and to shift the ground now was probably a tactical error, although difficult to avoid.[55] The indignation of opposition was voiced by Fox, who denounced this "scandalous, treacherous and disgraceful vote," and declared his intention of leaving parliament to the ministers.[56]

Once again the opposition had snatched defeat from the jaws of victory; and the circumstances strangely recall those of the Middlesex election. It was one thing to carry an abstract proposition in committee, but quite another to force the passage of specific legislation, especially if it touched the royal prerogative or the royal household. Sir George Savile later commented shrewdly on the success of these "declaratory and theoretic" resolutions, "not going directly to any effect.... People," he said, "love well-sounding and constitutional maxims.... It is

---

[54] *Correspondence of King George III*, V, No. 2991.
[55] *Letter to Lord North on his Re-election* (London, 1780).
[56] *Parliamentary History*, XXI:494 ff.

pleasanter to read fighting stories than to fight."[57] It was even suggested that the ministry used the Dunning resolutions as a safety valve
for discontent, knowing that the waverers, having thus satisfied the
frantic virtue of their constituents, could be relied on to defeat any
practical proposals.[58] This Machiavellian design may have been beyond the resources of political strategy at this time, but there can be
little doubt that in effect the end was achieved. The return of many
county members to the ministerial fold may have been as disgraceful
as Fox would have it, but there was another side to their recantation,
and it is necessary to turn again to the county meetings and their relation to whig politics.

So far as the county meetings and their association were designed
to promote the cause of reform, it was inevitable that there should
be differences of opinion about the degree in which reform should be
attempted. While there was a gradation of opinion from conservative
to radical, there are three main categories in which the advocates of
reform may be placed. The conservative wing, represented by Burke
and Rockingham, aimed at reducing ministerial patronage in parliament and at elections. Their views were expressed in Burke's bill for
economical reform, and involved no change in the electoral system.
Then came a second body of opinion, closely related to the former,
but regarded by most of the Rockingham whigs as too dangerous. This
favored reform in the representation of the existing electorate by such
measures as shorter parliaments, an increase in membership for the
counties, and possibly the abolition of some rotten boroughs. None
of the unrepresented population would be enfranchised, but the old
electorate of freeholders would gain greater control, especially in the
counties. A third group of reformers may properly be called radical,
for its program implied a complete departure from the old representation of property and advocated universal suffrage to insure the representation of persons. Its demands were usually coupled with those
for frequent parliaments and the reduction of patronage, as advocated
by the more conservative. This program gained ground as discussion
developed, but it never predominated. Thus the three groups may

---

[57] *Wyvill Papers,* III:328.
[58] *A Short History of the Last Session of Parliament* (London, 1780).

be considered as demanding, respectively, reform through the existing parliament, reform through the existing electorate, and reform through the enfranchisement of the unrepresented population.[59]

Early in the reform movement, the conservative program of economical—that is, administrative—reform was challenged by those who wished the campaign to include at least the shortening of the duration of parliaments and an increased membership for the counties. At the Wiltshire meeting in January, Sir William Jones expressed the opinion that reform could be insured only if parliament became more representative. Otherwise nothing would be easier than to undo later any administrative reforms that might now be gained. Shelburne and Fox both attended the meeting and gave a qualified assent to some kind of representational reform.[60]

The issue was squarely faced when the deputies from the counties met in the second week of March, that is, several weeks before Dunning's motion. The memorial approved at that meeting was directed at the restoration of parliamentary independence. Its first aim was the reduction of royal or ministerial control, and in this the delegates concurred entirely with the parliamentary whigs. But they did not stop here. They proceeded to recommend positive reforms by the addition of at least one hundred members for the counties, and by the requirement of triennial parliaments. In other words, the deputies represented the middle group of reformers who would change the structure of parliament without changing the electorate. Since they were seeking to restore that "independency" of legislature from executive which had been regarded by many as the chief security of a balanced constitution, they might well claim an authentic whig ancestry. But this did not give their program a clear passage. Already the hesitation of some counties became evident. The proposals were carried by 12 to 5 and by 11 to 6 of the delegations, one county, Hertfordshire, being willing to vote for the additional members but not to shorten

[59] While the distinction has usually been made between reforms restricted to reducing patronage and those involving an increase in the electorate, due attention has rarely been given to the intermediate program of reform. There is a vital difference between proposals for shorter parliaments and the transfer of members, and proposals to enfranchise new sections of the population.

[60] *The Remembrancer* (1780), p. 135; *Wyvill Papers*, I:108.

the duration of parliament.[61] Both reforms were therefore included in the form of association, and were acted upon by the county meetings which followed.

Many counties endorsed this platform, but there were ominous omissions, and even in those counties which accepted them the approval did not go unchallenged. At the York meeting Lord John Cavendish and Sir George Savile both expressed their dislike of additions to the original plan of economical reform, although the latter expressed his willingness to uphold the desires of his constituents.[62] Like the county of Hertford, Savile felt less uneasiness about the additional county members than about shorter parliaments, to which Burke's objection of 1770 still held good with many, namely, the excessive and ruinous competition with the treasury in election expenses. The dissentients, in fact, voiced the fears held still more strongly by Rockingham and Burke.

Rockingham himself had been uneasy on this matter since February. "My mind is by no means at ease," he wrote to a Yorkshire freeholder, "in regard to certain rumours respecting some vague and crude propositions" likely to be brought forward. "The grievances we feel, and the cause of our misfortune arise from the *corruption of men when chosen into Parliament*."[63] He could see only confusion from the adoption of speculative and visionary schemes.

His relative, Earl Fitzwilliam, also urged the Yorkshire electors to "adhere strictly to one object, to reduce the influence of the crown, as the true cause of every evil. In this every part of the kingdom seems united; but upon other objects you will certainly be divided. ... A better representation is not only desirable but in a manner necessary; but of all things the most difficult to be brought about. No plan, decently practicable, has yet been devised; and till such is ready, every public resolution upon the subject tends more to mischief than to good, because it alarms and does not satisfy."[64] Fitzwilliam was present at the Huntingdonshire meeting in April, and there he came out definitely against annual parliaments and all electoral changes. The Duke of

---

[61] *Wyvill Papers*, I:120–128.
[62] *The Remembrancer* (1780), p. 267; *Wyvill Papers*, I:148 ff.
[63] Albemarle, *op. cit.*, II:395.
[64] *Wyvill Papers*, IV:127 ff.

Manchester, also a leader of the Rockingham whigs, tried, according to a hostile critic, to prevent Fitzwilliam from taking his stand, but, once it was taken, Manchester felt himself so much in agreement that he supported him in it.[65]

Rockingham and Burke continued to express regret at the turn the campaign was taking.[66] In May, Burke spoke and voted against Sawbridge's motion for shorter parliaments, declaring that he thus gave a pledge of sincerity, in spite of his systematic opposition to the ministry.[67] Rockingham for his part wrote to a friend that abstract and speculative propositions would furnish everlasting discussion in the schools of Utopia, though meanwhile slight remedies would be enough to save England and her constitution.[68]

The Duke of Portland, another mainstay of the whigs, declined to attend the Buckinghamshire meeting on learning that triennial elections and the addition of a hundred county members would be voted on. He expressed the usual regrets that union was prevented by the injection of controversial proposals. He had, he said, always acted with a party, and he had hoped that by concentrating on the reduction of the influence of the crown the petitions might have achieved the formation of a party capable of resisting the torrent of corruption. He added another argument which deserves mention. The addition of more county members would, he declared, throw too much weight into the scale of the aristocracy. The representation of the counties would be engrossed by the most opulent families, and members would look for support to the great men and their retainers who could not safely be regarded as immune from the allurements of the crown. "I can no more let the aristocratical part preponderate over the democratical than I can suffer the royal influence to endanger the other two." And the duke ended on the familiar argument of Burke: "I am fearful of taking down any part of an old fabric, lest I bring the whole to the ground."[69]

Thus the cleavage appeared which destroyed the hope of a united

---

[65] *Correspondence of King George III*, V, No. 3000.

[66] Albemarle, *op. cit.*, II:402, 408; Fitzmaurice, *Life of Shelburne*, II:50; *Correspondence of Edmund Burke*, II:335.

[67] *Parliamentary History*, XXI:605.

[68] Albemarle, *op. cit.*, II:409.

[69] *Ibid.*, II:410–415.

front and revived the suspicion that partisan motives were supreme. Even Lord George Gordon must be regarded as a true prophet when he said that, without unanimity among themselves, opposition could do no service to the people.[70] Richard Watson, in spite of his frequent adherence to Rockingham, had proposed for the Cambridgeshire meeting a program of triennial parliaments and reform in the conduct of elections; and he later expressed the feelings of many moderate reformers when he wrote: "I differed in this opinion from some of those whom I considered as the first whigs of the country; but their arguments appeared to me to bear a temporizing cast.... Mr. Burke had much influence with them; I admired, as everybody did, the talents, but I did not admire the principles of that gentleman ... and his virulent abuse of Dr. Price persuaded me that he was a tory, perhaps indeed an aristocratic tory."[71] Some counties adopted plans of reform; others seceded from the movement, "We ... suspect," wrote one reforming chairman to Wyvill in Yorkshire, "that the Rockingham party have thrown this damp upon the ardor of the people; we are resolved if one set of men will not assist us to relinquish them totally, and adhere to those who will."[72]

Wyvill, however, refused to give up hope that the differences might be composed without abandoning the plan of reform. He pointed out that the nobility must naturally hesitate before committing themselves to a popular plan; and if their hesitation was treated with the candor and good nature to which the doubts of friends were always entitled, many of their number might still be won over.[73] There was in fact some evidence to support this view. Lord Effingham, one of the Yorkshire peers who acted with Rockingham, showed his liberal sympathies by accepting the Yorkshire plan of reform—triennial parliaments and the additional county members. Sir George Savile was perhaps a more notable convert. He was as skeptical of the merit of more frequent parliaments as of "washing one's shirt ever so often if the water be as dirty as the shirt";[74] but he was more hopeful of the addition to the number of county members. Another notable convert from the Rock-

---

[70] *Parliamentary History*, XXI:537–538.
[71] *Anecdotes of the Life of Richard Watson*, pp. 80–81.
[72] *Wyvill Papers*, III:193.
[73] *Ibid.*, pp. 194–195.   [74] *Ibid.*, p. 208.

ingham whigs was the Duke of Richmond, who went so far as to advocate not only annual parliaments, but the more revolutionary principle of manhood suffrage.

Universal suffrage appeared in the program of the Westminster committee in May, 1780. Earlier proposals, such as that of Jebb, had evaded the direct question of the nature of representation, and Burke had attacked the suggestion in parliament. "Popular election," he had declared, "is a mighty evil."[75] Now, however, the Westminster sub committee, appointed by the main committee to examine the possibility of free elections, came out strongly for universal suffrage, which, it declared, was essential, although obscured by "the undue preference that has been afforded to the rights of property." The committee submitted a scheme for a revised electoral system based upon the division of counties into constituencies approximately equal in population, and provided for voting rights in all male inhabitants, with the inevitable exception of criminal, minor, and insane.[76] Soon afterward, the Duke of Richmond introduced his plan of annual parliaments and universal suffrage, as outlined in this declaration.[77] Most of his whig colleagues had expressed their fears of much more conservative changes, probably foreseeing their extension into such radical proposals; and Richmond's motion came at a singularly inopportune time to quiet those fears, for the Gordon riots were plunging London into confusion, and were marking yet another turning point in favor of the ministry.

Thus by the end of the parliamentary session in June, 1780, the country gentlemen had shown that they were willing only to declare in vague terms for reform, but not to pass any important legislation to carry it out. The more ardent reformers were strengthening their hold on the county meetings, and particularly on the committees appointed by them to form "Mr. Wyvill's congress."[78] The Gordon riots increased the fears of the timid, and probably served the ministry well. When the king dissolved parliament, and forced an election in September, the whigs found that they had lost rather than gained ground. Sir George Savile could indeed boast that he had been elected by his con-

[75] *Parliamentary History*, XXI:603.
[76] *Wyvill Papers*, I:228 ff.
[77] *Parliamentary History*, XXI:686.
[78] *Correspondence of King George III*, V, No. 3291.

stituents instead of being returned in Lord Rockingham's drawing
room; but Burke was rejected by Bristol, and Hartley by Hull; and
Lord John Cavendish gave up his seat at York because he would not
accept the plan of reform. The bane of the whigs, Burke declared, was
the admitting of schemers and speculators to persuade the people that
they had designs on the constitution; and he lamented the variety of
opinion which separated Richmond from Savile—"the first men of
their age and country,"—and both from Rockingham and himself.[79]

While Burke thus mourned the disagreements among the friends
of Rockingham, those who took the liberal view voiced their exasperation at the conservative leaders. In December, Jebb prophesied that the
whigs would make an effort in the following February, and if that
failed, they would be ready to join the reformers on a basis of cordiality.[80] Others were less patient. "For God's sake," wrote Lord Mahon
to Wyvill, "let us be well aware of *even seeming* to concede any
further.... Nothing but firmness can procure us the united support
of opposition."[81] "I love Burke," Barré told Shelburne; "I admire
him, even in his wanderings, but when those wanderings come to be
adopted seriously and obstinately by men of far higher description
than himself, then they become alarming indeed." The Duke of Richmond, Barré went on, had worked night and day to persuade Rockingham to accept the plan of reform, but "Rockingham's indecision
was not to be cured by crabbed conversations or messages in town."[82]
"Is it not almost incredible," Shelburne replied, "that the head of the
whigs, as he styles himself, should not be moved by resentment, rival-
ship, the call of his country, the conduct of his friends, particularly
Sir George Savile, to be a whit more decisive than when he set out,
and still there he stands, obstinately stopping the free course of popular spirit, which alone can ever oppose the court."[83]

Such indignation with the moderate and hesitating policy of Rockingham is intelligible, but it does less than justice to the whig position.
To an intense individualist like Chatham or Shelburne nothing was
more simple than to decide on a course of action and expect others to
accept and follow it. Rockingham, on the other hand, was the leader

---

[79] *Correspondence of Edmund Burke*, II:381 ff.
[80] *Wyvill Papers*, IV:499.   [82] Fitzmaurice, *Life of Shelburne*, II:68.
[81] *Ibid.*, III:276.   [83] *Ibid.*, p. 72.

of a group, the representative of a party, before the history of party had accumulated the experience of technique. He was accustomed at every turn to seek the interest and the opinions of those who acted with him. When in addition the leader was a man of hesitating and conservative temper, the consequences were indecisive. Of his many advisers Burke held the greatest ascendancy, and Rockingham rarely acted contrary to Burke's advice. There were, however, other counsels which might, temporarily at least, serve to divert whig policy, if not to direct it. Such was the baffling influence of Charles Fox.

Fox was not in origin one of the main corps of whigs; but after the American war had begun he gravitated steadily toward Rockingham and his friends, and by this constant association in opposition Fox came to be regarded as a whig leader. "I have never given you the least hint of advice," Burke told him in October, 1777, "about joining yourself in a declared connection with our Party, nor do I now; yet, as I love that Party very well, and am clear that you are better able to serve them than any man I know, I wish that things should be so kept as to leave you mutually very open to one another in all changes and contingencies."[84] "Believe me, my dear Lord," Fox wrote to Rockingham in November, 1778, "though I certainly disapprove of some things which you have done, and of many more which you have left undone, yet there is no man in this country who wishes more heartily to agree with you in everything, or who is more convinced that the salvation of this country must ultimately depend upon you and your friends."[85] Fox was a great parliamentarian, and his assistance could be of the first importance to the whigs; though, as a clever politician, he might well add to those suspicions of partisan self-interest which were always the bane of the whig reputation. Perhaps the best clue to his position in the party is found in a comment attributed to Lord Frederick Cavendish in 1780. "Our body," he said, "has property . . . but we have not those powers that enable men to take the lead in public assemblies. You see what has been the case of C. Fox. We must naturally give way to such men."[86] It was a repetition of 1769.

Fox was more outspoken in defense of popular and American rights

---

[84] *Letter to the Hon. Charles James Fox* (Oct. 8, 1777).
[85] Albemarle, *op. cit.*, II:370.
[86] Fitzmaurice, *Life of Shelburne*, II:70.

than the average whig. But he was also unwilling to resign himself to exclusion from power, and he urged Rockingham to take up a less intransigent position. After Saratoga he was regarded by those close to the ministry as one who could easily be won over, although possibly more dangerous as an ally than as an opponent.[87] In 1778 he had sponsored a ministerial scheme by which the whigs should come into office with North and Thurlow; but Rockingham and the Cavendishes killed the proposal.[88] After this failure he had expressed himself at length to Rockingham on whig policy. "What you considered as a step of the most dangerous tendency to the whig party, I looked upon as a most favourable opportunity for restoring it to that power and influence which I wish it to have as earnestly as you can do.... Our difference of opinion is quite complete. You think you can best serve the country by continuing in a fruitless opposition; I think it impossible to serve it at all but by coming into power.... I do beg of you, my dear Lord, to consider how very impracticable it is either for me or for many other parts of the Opposition, to go on together upon the ideas upon which you maintain your refusal. For is it, or is it not, a fair and open declaration that you will never have anything to do with any ministry that is *not entirely* of your framing? ... I do not mention this as a matter of reproach, but only to show you how very impossible it is for anybody who is not *one of you* to enter into your ideas and objects of opposition." Fox went on to ask if Rockingham would persist in resisting all such proposals, and, if so, whether he would countenance a joint arrangement to the extent of allowing his friends to serve in it if they wished.[89]

It was Richmond who replied to Fox's letter, and he set forth with admirable clarity the aims and policy of the Rockingham whigs in considering ministerial negotiations. Their refusal, he said, was not based upon the desire to enforce a complete monopoly of power. The difficulty was that, if they combined with even a few of the old ministry, it would be impossible to disown the policy of that ministry as thoroughly as it ought to be disowned for a fresh start. Moreover, in

---

[87] Auckland MSS (Brit. Mus.), III, fol. 395 (Wm. Eden to Lord North, Dec. 7, 1777).

[88] Albemarle, *op. cit.*, II:353–355.

[89] Albemarle, *op. cit.*, II:371; Russell, *Memorials and Correspondence of Charles James Fox,* I:206.

such circumstances, unlike those of a complete change of ministers, some clear agreement was necessary beforehand to indicate the extent to which measures could be adopted which the whigs thought highly desirable. No such indications had been given either for domestic or foreign affairs.[90]

During the later months of 1779 the attitude of the Rockingham whigs was but part of a complicated situation of dissatisfaction and intrigue. The death of Suffolk and the resignation of Gower had left two groups leaderless within the ministry; and both were determined to turn the misfortunes and hesitation of North to their own advantage. In particular the Bedford whigs were eager to restore their ascendancy by substituting Gower for North as head of the government. The king desired, as always, to form a strong administration with the support of all groups and the domination of none. He was willing, but not anxious, to sacrifice North if necessary. By November the position was critical. The new parliamentary session was confronted with serious trouble in Ireland and mounting unrest at home. Negotiations with the opposition were again set on foot, but in the hands of Thurlow they may hardly be regarded as disingenuous. While Thurlow was ostensibly seeking the broad administration desired by the king, he himself also represented the desire of the Bedford whigs for a government in which they should play the decisive part; and they were not anxious to clear the ground for a Rockingham administration.[91]

The Rockingham whigs could obtain no assurance that their wishes regarding either policy or personnel would he respected, and they had no intention of bolstering the power of existing ministers or of other advisers whom they suspected of special influence in the royal closet. "It is evident to me," the king wrote, "what treatment I am to expect from Opposition if I was to call them now to my service; nothing less will satisfy them than a total change of measures and men; to obtain their support I must deliver up my person, my principles, and my dominions into their hands; I must also abandon every old, illustrious

---

[90] Russell, *Memorials and Correspondence of Charles James Fox*, I:213.

[91] H. Butterfield, "Lord North and Mr. Robinson, 1779," *Cambridge Historical Journal*, V:255–279; *Correspondence of King George III*, IV, Nos. 2875, 2894; Egerton MSS 2232, fol. 25.

and faithful servant I have to be treated as their resentment or their mercy may incline them. . . . Nothing therefore remains for me to do, but to exert myself and to call upon those who serve me to exert themselves in support of my legal authority, and to resist this formidable and desperate opposition."[92] The king was confirmed in his stand by Jenkinson's report that although the people wanted a stronger government, they had no good opinion of the opposition, and did not wish for its success as a party.[93] Efforts to attract support continued, but there was no serious intention of giving in to the whig demands.

By June, 1780, however, the whig campaign seemed to have spent itself. The country gentlemen had proved a broken reed; the county associations had fallen into radical hands; and the Gordon riots discredited the idea of change, while strengthening the reputation of king and ministry. The Rockingham group had in fact rallied strongly to the cause of law and order; and this, together with the obvious division between the more radical and conservative sections of opposition, seems to have tempted the administration to a new negotiation, conducted through Frederick Montagu, a respected friend of Rockingham.

Obscure as are the details of this negotiation, they form an essential part of the history of the Rockingham whigs and anticipate their position in March, 1782. It seems that Rockingham was now willing to allow his principal adherents to serve under North in a reconstituted ministry. It is even possible that the clamor for parliamentary reform had led him to consider whether an alliance with North would not be more congenial than one with Shelburne, whose popular sympathies were obvious. As early as April, Fox and North had been in consultation;[94] and late in June, North and Montagu were in close conference, amid increasing rumors of coalition. The opposition referred to the negotiation as if it had been begun by Lord North, while Charles Jenkinson spoke to the king of the "advances made by opposition." There was probably a tentative readiness on both sides.[95]

---

[92] *Correspondence of King George III*, IV, No. 2882.
[93] *Ibid.*, IV, No. 2895.
[94] *Ibid.*, V, No. 2993.
[95] Russell, *Memorials and Correspondence of Charles James Fox*, I:254; *Correspondence of King George III*, V, No. 3080.

In laying down the conditions under which he might come into office, Rockingham carefully refrained from discussing the headship of the treasury; although Montagu probably emphasized to North the general whig desire for Rockingham's own leadership. Lord Sandwich was the only member of the ministry whose resignation was demanded. He must go, and Keppel must replace him at the admiralty; while Richmond should be a secretary of state, probably with Fox. "Great parts" of the proposals for economical reform must be conceded. There must be no royal veto on American independence. Actual policy on this point would have to depend on circumstances.[96]

These conditions were obviously unacceptable to the king. Fearing the constitutional "wildness" of opposition, he was not satisfied with evasion on American policy, even though it were interpreted to mean that the whigs would continue at least a passive war. He refused to sacrifice Sandwich for Keppel, and his refusal on this point was largely responsible for the breakdown of negotiations.[97] He would admit Fox and Richmond to office only upon conditions. "There seems to be a decisive disinclination," wrote Rockingham, "to almost every idea on which (I thought) a government, either in regard to measures or persons, could be formed."[98]

Once again the whigs had fallen between two stools. Rockingham could be suspected of a readiness to give up the long struggle. The high ground of dissociation from an unsuccessful ministry seemed to have been abandoned, and the cause of America relegated to mere expediency. Suspicion of Shelburne had been advertised, and Shelburne himself deeply offended. However justifiable this may have been from his own point of view, Rockingham could be regarded as having made too much of it, while accepting overtures from North.

These negotiations of 1780 may have been affected to some extent by Rockingham's own indisposition and weariness. They were none the less ominous for the future. The Duke of Richmond, in spite of the use freely made of his name—and of the fact that Rockingham had

---

[96] I. R. Christie, "The Marquis of Rockingham and Lord North's Offer of a Coalition, June–July, 1780," *English Historical Review*, LXIX (1954): 388–407.
[97] Add. MSS 38,214 (Liverpool Papers, XXV), fol. 59.
[98] Albermarle, *op. cit.*, II:420–421.

apparently kept him informed—declared afterwards that he had had
nothing to do with "that strange negotiation." The Cavendishes were
not happy in the ascendancy of Fox, and suggested that Shelburne
might well become their natural leader.[90] Thus the affair foreshad-
owed the rift between Fox and Shelburne, and even the eventual
coalition with North. When Shelburne expressed his exasperation in
December, 1780, he was thinking not only of Rockingham's refusal
to accept the radical program, but also of the apparent weakening of
whig resolution, the imminence of whig discord, and the insult to
himself. He had assumed the mantle of Chatham.

Opposition, according to Shelburne, was once more composed of
a great number of petty squads of individuals whose conduct had defeated the purpose of a united opposition.[100] From among the friends
of Rockingham the Duke of Richmond felt keenly the same dissatisfaction. "The few," he wrote to his leader, "who are capable of any
exertion are split into miserable little palliating politics, unable to act
together, un-united upon any system."[101] And whereas some of the
great whig magnates were content to lament, Richmond was more
eager. Amid the despondent lethargy which afflicted the whigs during
the year 1781, he attempted to achieve unanimity by cordial relations
with Shelburne and the other friends of Chatham.

In the autumn of 1781, the Yorkshire committee of association
adopted a second address setting forth the various projects of reform
and treating with some sympathy the different points of view.[102] The
committee, however, stood firm on its previous policy of recommending more frequent parliaments and the addition of one hundred members of parliament for the counties. Many reformers regarded the
omission of an extended suffrage as too conservative, but they were
willing to compromise thus far with friendly whigs.[103] On this platform, therefore, emended by Rockingham if necessary, Shelburne proposed that opposition should unite for the parliamentary campaign
of 1781–82. Alternatively, he said, if Rockingham would suggest "any

[90] Fitzmaurice, *Life of Shelburne*, II:66, 70.
[100] *Parliamentary History*, XXI:1025–1026.
[101] Albemarle, *op. cit.*, II:429–430.
[102] *A Second Address from the Committee of Association of the County of York* (York,
n.d.).
[103] *Wyvill Papers*, IV:512.

other radical and effectual plan, which would unite and satisfy the friends of the country both within doors and without, he would be willing to co-operate with Lord Rockingham upon such ground; that he wished never to see more than *two* parties; that of the Crown and that of the People." According to Shelburne's own account, "Lord Rockingham, after having been pressed for two days, refused to accede to any of the three above-mentioned propositions; but had no plan of his own whatever to propose. A union on the ground of the American war was the only idea suggested by Lord Rockingham; which was thought much too vague, too weak, as well as too inadequate to the situation of the country for Lord Shelburne to accede to."[104]

In short, the familiar story was once more repeated. Rockingham fully shared Burke's inveterate dislike of theoretical or radical proposals, and he was now firmly rooted in the ground that had been taken up in 1769. Opposition was to be carried on, but confined to the immediate issue of practical politics. This "contracted field of operations" happened now to be conciliation with America. "I highly approve," wrote Richmond, "of the attempt to get rid of the American war anyhow, and do believe it a point on which the nation generally will be of our opinion."[105] So, vague and weak as this seemed to Shelburne in the light of constructive policy, it was the sole aim of whig concentration.

It happened that just as the resolve was taken to attack only the conduct and continuation of the war in America, news came of the defeat of Cornwallis at Yorktown; and the whigs had scarcely to fight. Indeed, it is true of the fall of North that, as a recent writer has said of the events of 1780, "the strength of the parliamentary opposition was to a great degree the register rather than the cause of the weakness of a ministry";[106] and it is more correct to say that the government failed than that the opposition succeeded. There is nothing in the events of 1781 to justify the claim that the whigs encompassed the defeat of Lord North or the king. The ministry disintegrated from within, and the failure of the war was also its own failure.

For the present purpose much significance attaches to the actual

[104] Fitzmaurice, *Life of Shelburne,* II:82.
[105] Albemarle, *op. cit.,* II:439.   [106] Butterfield, *op. cit.,* p. 272.

terms on which the king replaced the old ministers by new. Did he in fact surrender to that "desperate and formidable opposition" which he so hated? And in particular did he yield to the pressure of party, represented by the corps of Rockingham whigs?

After Yorktown most of the independent members of parliament, and some influential sections of the ministry, realized that the war could not go on. Only the resolution of the king, supported by such responsible leaders as Sandwich and Germain, prevented immediate collapse; and these leaders were the objects of concerted attack from within the cabinet and from without. Ministerial majorities dwindled and at last were reversed on February 27 by the success of Conway's motion against the further prosecution of "an offensive war in America"—a motion carefully worded to win the maximum of support. The king was now obliged to consider the replacement of ministers; and although Lord North managed to avert votes of censure by small majorities on the 8th and 15th of March, on the 20th he announced the fall of his long-lived administration. The question of successors was urgent.

While ministerial groups had been divided on the practicability of continuing the war, the opposition was not innocent of disagreement on the same issue. It may be that Shelburne disliked to make America the common ground of opposition because of his reluctance to admit the complete independence of the colonies. It is true that by January, 1781, he had accepted the inevitable, and had expressed his preference for separation rather than a dependence imposed by force against the constitution;[107] but he confessed to having been a very Quixote on the subject. At the opening of parliament in the following November— that is, after Yorktown—he had declared that the question of American independence was a weighty question, not to be easily decided. On February 7, 1782, he reminded the House that his principles on the subject were well known; he had repeated from year to year "that he never would consent, under any possible circumstances to acknowledge the independence of America. . . . He was known to differ from his most intimate friends and respectable connexions on the subject."[108]

---

[107] *Parliamentary History*, XXI:1035.
[108] *Ibid.*, XXII:987.

The ancient stumbling block which had prevented union under Chatham now hindered the final onslaught. It was even suggested that the few ministers who were anxious to prosecute the war with America were fortified by the knowledge of some sympathy in the ranks of opposition.[109]

Thus when the necessity faced the king of forming a more popular ministry, he was again encouraged by North to hope that he might divide the opposition so as to take in only a part of it with some of the existing ministers.[110] On this basis negotiations began in earnest after Conway's motion against the war in America. The first step was, naturally enough, to win back the Bedford group, lost only recently and partially to the king's policy. Gower, their leader, undertook to approach the Duke of Grafton, next in order of presumed accessibility. The basis of a Gower ministry would be the retention of existing possessions in America. The result of the consultation between Grafton and Gower was the recognition that they could not form a government;[111] and the king proceeded, very reluctantly, to look farther afield. Negotiations were entrusted mainly to Lord Chancellor Thurlow.

As the agent of the king, Thurlow represented the desire for a nonpartisan administration; and he had already discussed this possibility with Shelburne, who stood for the same policy. Thurlow, however, recognized the difficulty of forming a new ministry without the Rockingham whigs, the champions of party, and he sought therefore to tone down royal emphasis on Shelburne's "lack of connection."[112] Moreover, as North reminded the king, Thurlow was held in high estimation by the opposition, and the Rockingham whigs shared his fear of popular movements. If, therefore, the rift between Shelburne and Rockingham was too wide for a joint administration, it would appear possible for Thurlow and Rockingham to unite and "oppose a firm barrier against any dangerous popular measures."[113] In these circumstances Thurlow approached Rockingham, a move criticized by George III as doomed to failure by starting in the most hostile quarter.

---

[109] *A Word at Parting to the Earl of Shelburne* (London, 1782).
[110] *Correspondence of King George III*, V, No. 3535.
[111] *Ibid.*, Nos. 3537, 3545.
[112] *Ibid.*, No. 3542.   [113] *Ibid.*, No. 3545.

Rockingham, warned by Richmond that the approach was not wholly genuine, laid down several essentials for his entry into office. He asked for the assurance of royal assent to American independence, Burke's establishment bill, most of the contractors' bill, and some lesser administrative reforms in a program of peace and economy. Should these requirements be met, Rockingham was prepared to consider the formation of a government. But he would treat only with the king on a basis of direct and complete responsibility. The king on his side would yield full confidence only to a nonpartisan ministry. He would not surrender to Rockingham. "My language," he reminded Thurlow, "went to a broad bottom, not the delivering myself up to a party." "The changing from one party to another can answer no real good."[114]

The breach was obviously too wide for immediate agreement. Thurlow urged Rockingham to let his program follow entry into office, rather than demand it as a preliminary condition. Rockingham declined to form a ministry first, and then agree on its measures.[115] North insisted that the king must send for either Rockingham or Shelburne, and Thurlow transferred his attentions to Shelburne as the more likely recruit.[116] At this stage the ministry resigned. Shelburne, like Rockingham, would deal only directly with the king; and an interview was accordingly arranged,[117]

Shelburne had made it amply clear that he would be no party to an administration which did not include the Rockingham whigs. "You can stand without me," he is alleged to have told Rockingham, "but I could not without you";[118] and now, armed with some measure of grudging royal confidence, he approached the task of winning Rockingham's adherence to a joint administration. Rockingham refused to defer his program until the ministry had been formed, and there seemed a danger that the negotiations would break down. At this stage some of Rockingham's friends grew alarmed and urged him to coöperate with Shelburne. Warning them of the danger, he yielded to their entreaties, but still insisted that the whig coalition must be

[114] Albemarle, *op. cit.*, II:446; *Correspondence of King George III*, V, Nos. 3555, 3563–3564.

[115] Egerton MSS (Brit. Mus.), 2232, fols. 46–50.

[116] *Correspondence of King George III*, V, No. 3566; Egerton MSS 2232, fol. 54.

[117] *Correspondence of King George III*, Nos. 3568, 3571.

[118] Horace Walpole, *Last Journals*, II:523.

founded on the prior acceptance of his main conditions. On this point he was supported by his friends, and Shelburne gave way.[119] He was able to assure Rockingham that the conditions previously laid down would be met; and he eventually succeeded in winning the king's gratitude by persuading Rockingham to avoid pressing his advantage in individual cases of dismissal from offices near the king. By March 27 the new ministry was formed, with Rockingham at the treasury, Shelburne secretary of state, and Thurlow the sole survivor of the king's friends.

Rockingham had not conceded any major part of his program; but he had accepted Shelburne as intermediary and colleague, chosen by the king. George III thus retained the substance of his demand for a ministry broader than party. In fact, the new government was a coalition, in which Rockingham was not so much prime minister as senior partner with Shelburne, and less trusted by the king. By the time the whigs came into office, their divisions were manifest. They differed on the desirability, and even the expediency, of American independence; on the role of the crown, and the place of party in government; and on parliamentary reform. If they should fall out, as it seemed they must, the first steps had already been taken toward a coalition with North. The whigs had gained little since the 'sixties, except experience.

---

[119] Richard Champion, *Comparative Reflections on the Past and Present . . . State of Great Britain* (London, 1787), chap. vii.

V. CONCLUSION

THE EARLY history of political party in England is often assumed to have the same characteristics as in the later Victorian and Edwardian period, when a relatively settled order was based on the alternation in power of two permanent groups. A more accurate analogy may be found in the history of the United States, where constitutional development proceeded from a point very similar to that of the Glorious Revolution. Executive and legislature were balanced in a constitution based on the principles of Locke, and political parties appeared, not in an alternating two-party system, but following one another in sequence. In effect, one party enjoyed a long reign of supreme power, declined, and was succeeded by a new, arising partly from its own ranks and partly from elements hitherto unrepresented. This new party in turn gained a virtual monopoly, and eventually yielded to yet a third, similarly constituted, and not to be mistaken for its predecessor in opposition. This converging and diverging process characterized whiggism and toryism in the eighteenth century. The older toryism died in the first half of the century, whiggism in the second. But the systems were recreated and the names survived.

There is a similarity between the two periods. The revolution and the Hanoverian settlement deprived the tories of their divinely sanctioned order represented by crown and church, and left them with only a traditional association and a vague belief in the nation as a structural unity. Whiggism, which had been the creed of limitation and resistance, became the accepted doctrine of parliamentary power, and the whigs monopolized the government.

Whiggism under George III suffered much the same fate as toryism after 1714. The king, using the great resources of the monarchy, succeeded in building his own parliamentary majority by absorbing the strongest features of both creeds. He accepted much of the whig theory of parliamentary supremacy, and took over the whig technique of management. At the same time he used the appeal of monarchy to rally support from tory and independent ranks which still cherished the illusion of a unified state free from the weakness of faction. A new toryism emerged, with a personnel differing from the old and in fact drawing largely from the whigs, just as they had won recruits from the expiring toryism of the past. By the second decade of his reign the whigs were but a remnant, and whiggism but a vague tradition of resistance to arbitrary power. Exposed to this onslaught on their aristocratic stronghold, they were simultaneously confronted by a new movement from the left. Political radicalism appeared, armed with a liberal interpretation of Locke, proclaiming the sovereignty of the people outside of parliament and demanding a drastic change in the representative system. On this vital question the whigs were divided. Many of their leaders could not forsake the comfortable security of property and influence for the speculative future of popular leadership, and clung, therefore, to a conservatism which became less and less distinguishable from the new tory creed. If they would not go forward, they must go back.

For a while they temporized. Unable to agree on great matters of policy, they emphasized the principle and the practice of party. They possessed the resources of a small but powerful aristocratic group, which, led by Rockingham and later by Portland, demonstrated the aristocratic virtues of loyalty and independence at their best. Including among their number "men of Spanish honour and Roman virtue,"[1] they could draw upon the ancient whig tradition of political liberty. If that tradition had been dimmed by the complacency of power, the illiberal acts of the king's ministers enabled it to regain some of its luster. They had in Edmund Burke a servant and ally whose conspicuous loyalty was matched by genius.[2] As an organizer he kept them together and mobilized their resources. He transformed their very weakness into strength, and their hesitation into a program of conservatism. Their inability to agree on constitutional principles became in his hands the refusal to accept theoretical reasoning as the basis for practical policy. Their habit of personal connection was elevated by him into an aristocratic responsibility for political leadership and the justification of government by party. Thus while the Rockingham

---

[1] *The Address of the People of Great Britain to the Inhabitants of America* (London, 1775), p. 31.

[2] "One on whom the thoroughest dependence may be given, where an obligation is owned."—Grafton to Chatham, Oct. 17, 1766, *Correspondence of William Pitt, Earl of Chatham* (London, 1839), III:111.

whigs were inherently incapable of becoming a party in the modern sense, they fought a battle for the system the profits of which they themselves could not enjoy. Throughout their long period of opposition they remained loyal to one another, and were recognized more definitely than any previous group as the nucleus of an alternative administration. There was, in their treatment by North, even a slight suggestion of the future status of His Majesty's Opposition.[3]

In their campaign against the king they fought mainly for two related principles the attainment of which would at the same time satisfy their own political interests and the sound whig practice of limited monarchy. The first of these was to prevent the executive power of the crown from being exercised, or policy determined, by any other persons than the ostensible ministers responsible to parliamentary criticism. This aim, which was formulated by Burke in 1770 (and which elevated whig hatred of Lord Bute almost to a constitutional principle), was not capable of being attained definitely and directly; for as long as the king held real power he could not be prevented from taking advice where he chose. The significance of Burke's accusation lies less in the failure to press it home than in the fact that it could reasonably be made, and that it was possible for the whigs to stir up sufficient agitation to deter a prudent king.

Their second aim was that of maintaining a coherent parliamentary group with an avowed program—a group whose members should take office only as a cabinet under their chosen leader, not as individuals selected by the king. This basic principle of party was a direct challenge to the king's privilege of choosing his own ministers; but the fight with George III was not carried to a finish. For whereas Rockingham in 1782 and Portland in 1783 both laid down their own terms and their own ministerial arrangements, on each occasion the king conducted the negotiations through a third person—Shelburne in 1782 and North in 1783—and on each occasion the new government was a coalition. The whigs failed to establish their principle of cabinet gov-

---

[3] H. W. C. Davis, *The Age of Grey and Peel* (Oxford, 1929), p. 11. On two occasions North notified Burke of the government's impending motions. It may be remarked, however, that on both occasions he had particular reasons for conciliatory behavior. At the time of the first (Feb. 19, 1775), he was about to introduce his conciliatory American propositions; and, in the summer of 1780, proposals for a joint administration were in process.

ernment. They were succeeded by a minister congenial to the king, and the long administration of the younger Pitt left the controversy in abeyance while the whigs quarreled among themselves.

Meanwhile, by placing such emphasis on the principle and practice of systematic party, as well as by their conservative interpretation of whiggism, the Rockingham whigs put themselves in the position of an exclusive group concerned primarily to obtain and monopolize power. Before the end of the war, the party which in the 'sixties had been the party of youth could be accused of closing its ranks against younger men. No young man of talents, declared a ministerial pamphleteer of 1780, had for years back met with the patronage of a minority long directed by a few veteran orators jealous of the recruits they needed.[4] The same conservative and partisan attitude antagonized Chatham and Shelburne, whose belief in nonpartisan administration was essentially the same as that of the king. The rift could not be closed. Even Rockingham considered the alternative possibility of a union with North; and with his death in 1782 the ascendancy of Fox effectually prevented the party from submitting to Shelburne. Party, in fact, triumphed over principle. The whigs entered into a fatal coalition with North, and this product of expediency and personal ambition could not but revive the suspicion that new party was but old faction writ large. "The great whig families," wrote Horace Walpole in 1783, "have lost all credit in their own counties."[5] The coalition was too much even for some of their own number; their loyalty would not stretch so far. Sir George Savile, the sure barometer of all that was best in whig independence and integrity, registered the division in the party. "Although I grant that nothing in this world is to be done by solitary efforts," he wrote to Hartley, "and that, if a man will not be content with being a well meaning non-effective, he must not be sentimentally nice about his accomplices,—yet, there is reason and measure in this as in all other things. . . . To unite as allies generally with men one ought to impeach, to act with a man who has done more mischief in a given time than one would have thought could have been well contrived, . . . to join cordially with such a man, can be justified but one

---

[4] *Common-place Arguments against Administration* . . . (3d ed.; Dublin, 1780), pp. 18–19.

[5] *Letters*, ed. Mrs. Paget Toynbee (Oxford, 1905), XIII:141–142.

way (if it can at all) viz. the lesser of two evils. . . . I say, if it can at all, because there is a third way, and that is, not cutting in at all."[6] These were the words of a wise and liberal whig, who realized that by refusing to go again into the wilderness the party was sacrificing its claim to represent the liberties of the people.

The American policy of the Rockingham whigs was determined in large part by this domestic controversy, in which they were determined to preserve the middle ground of aristocratic influence from the assaults of the new toryism on the one hand and an emerging radicalism on the other.

There were two main aspects of the American Revolution which the whigs had to face. The first was the essential whiggism of the colonial cause, especially in its earlier stages. American whigs demanded the same rights of property and trade, the same respect for charters, and the same control of taxation which had been the backbone of whiggism in seventeenth-century England. As Richard Watson declared in 1776, "it was a part of the nation which then resisted the king, because he would have taken from them their property, without their consent given by themselves or their representatives; and now it is a part of the empire which resists the legislature for the very same reason." English whigs could not refuse a measure of sympathy to this reflection of their own struggles. The American cause, declared Fox, "was the cause of freedom, the cause of the constitution, the cause of whiggism"; and even to Burke the Americans stood "in the same relation to England as England did to King James the Second in 1688. . . . So circumstanced, he certainly never could and never did wish the colonists to be subdued by arms."[7]

To Chatham this essential constitutionality of the American cause was the dominant consideration, and his sympathy was wholehearted until independence became a practical program. He was not greatly agitated by the other aspect of the Revolution, its attack on parliamentary supremacy. Parliament was to him but one of the great institutions

---

[6] Richard Warner, *Literary Recollections* (London, 1830), II:243–244; see also *Anecdotes of the Life of Richard Watson* (London, 1817), pp. 104–105.

[7] Richard Watson, *The Principles of the Revolution Vindicated* (Cambridge, 1776), p. 12; *Parliamentary History*, XXII:612; Edmund Burke, *An Appeal from the New to the Old Whigs.*

of a great commercial empire with a unity and a power which he was determined to preserve. He was not afraid either of the crown or of a broader electorate. The Rockingham whigs, however, interpreted their creed in the light of established parliamentary influence, the source of their own political leadership. In their eyes the challenge to parliament was of far more serious import. Parliament was the supreme government of the empire, and its authority could not be shaken in America without suffering at home. The colonies attempted first to restrict and then to disown this authority, in the name of communities outside the represented class. They were therefore manifestly radical in their relation to established constitutional practice. Like their friends the parliamentary reformers, they could claim the mantle of Locke, but the whigs had no desire to surrender their long prescription of power in favor of a primitive interpretation of whig theory. They were the champions of political liberty, but they preferred that liberty in its authorized English translation.

Torn between the two forces in American resistance, the Rockingham whigs sought to confine the ground of opposition as narrowly as possible to immediate issues. The actual measures of the king's ministry must be attacked, but no opening must be given for the more radical exponents of opposition in England or in America. Especially must the American problem be regarded as an outcome of ministerial folly and a direct result of the policy of George III. As long as the emphasis was on the ministry, and not on parliament, the whigs could support Chatham's assertion of whig rights in the colonies, even though they might not go so far as to rejoice in American resistance. They could also use the Stuart parallel of tyranny and arbitrary rule if the king's ministers were held closely to their responsibility for the disorders.

Throughout the course of American resistance the whigs played variations on this theme. In the early days of the Stamp Act they abated the disturbances by practical repeal which did not disown the right of supremacy. When the policy of coercion began they opposed it as a practical error due to ministerial incompetence, and they sought to prevent parliament from being drawn into the measures of restraint. Responsibility was fixed on particular ministers who owed their position to particular abuses of established constitutional practice. By 1776 this attempt to dissociate parliament had failed. After a period of despondency, the whigs began to consider American independence as a preferable alternative to dependence on the crown. From the unsuccessful military campaigns they gained a fresh opportunity to focus blame on the government, and, though looked at askance for their American principles, they spent the remaining years of opposition in belaboring the ministers for their misconduct of the war.

By this concentration on ministerial incompetence the whigs sought to avoid the embarrassing questions of parliamentary authority or radical reform. But these questions could not be avoided entirely. Suspicion without, and controversy within their ranks, hampered their effectiveness, while the very absence of a formulated policy seemed weak and inadequate against the strength of new toryism. It emphasized the personnel of party and revived the cry of faction. It bequeathed to the historian an uneasy inquiry whether America was not used as a stick to beat the ministry for faults committed at home; whether the whigs, in the safe irresponsibility of opposition, did not minimize the uncongeniality of the great affair which they took up "as a business." Had they been in office, the whigs might, it is true, have found a happier solution than war for the American problem; but that problem undoubtedly contained the same contradiction which beset their policy at home. Only for a time could they postpone making their choice between the acceptance of radical change and a surrender to the new toryism which embodied so much of established whig practice from the age of Walpole.

The outbreak of the French Revolution forced a decision. Compelled to choose between the excesses of liberty exemplified in France and its repression in England, the whig party, weakened by opportunism, broke up on a principle. Portland struggled long to preserve the solidarity which had been the bulwark of whig resistance to the king; but he could not hold the party together, and eventually in 1794 he took the road which brought him full circle to tory leadership. Fox led the liberal wing in the direction of the future, while Burke in his own person restored to toryism the great conceptions of conservative policy and an organic state.

INDEX